Turn

ALSO BY
ANNE TRUITT

Daybook: The Journal of an Artist

VIKING

Turn

THE

JOURNAL

OF AN

ARTIST

Anne Truitt

VIKING

Viking Penguin Inc., 40 West 23rd Street,
New York, New York 10010, U.S.A.
Penguin Books Ltd, Harmondsworth,
Middlesex, England
Penguin Books Australia Ltd, Ringwood,
Victoria, Australia
Penguin Books Canada Limited, 2801 John Street,
Markham, Ontario, Canada L3R 1B4
Penguin Books (N.Z.) Ltd, 182-190 Wairau Road,
Auckland 10, New Zealand

First published in 1986 by Viking Penguin Inc.
Published simultaneously in Canada

Grateful acknowledgment is made to
Anne Buchanan Crosby and Louise Dean for
permission to reprint their letters to the author.

LIBRARY OF CONGRESS CATALOGING IN PUBLICATION DATA
Truitt, Anne, 1921–
Turn: the journal of an artist.
1. Truitt, Anne, 1921– —Diaries.
2. Artists—United States—Diaries.
I. Title. N6537.T73A2 1986   709'.2'4 [B]   85-41099
ISBN 0-670-81175-0

Printed in the United States of America by
R. R. Donnelley & Sons Company, Harrisonburg, Virginia
Design by Elissa Ichiyasu
Set in Garamond

For the memory of
my mother and my father,
and for my grandchildren

ACKNOWLEDGMENTS

A large part of this book was written at Yaddo. I am grateful to Curtis Harnack, the executive director of Yaddo, and to the board of directors and the staff of Yaddo for their trust in me, and for their personal loyalty while I was acting executive director of Yaddo for nine months in 1984.

I am grateful to Ramon Osuna for his generosity in giving me a trip to Europe, and to Annelise Seidenfaden for her abundant and imaginative hospitality in Italy.

I thank Dorothy Orio for her careful work in typing my manuscript.

I thank my sister Louise Crelly for her affectionate sensitivity.

I thank Margot Backas for her wise counsel. My editor, Nan Graham, has brought to the entire process of this book her experience, her intelligence, and her acute sensibility; her generous enthusiasm has been a source of pleasure as well as support.

My children, Alexandra, Mary, and Sam, have enhanced my life with their lovely loyalty while I was writing. The companionship of my grandchildren is a grace note in my life.

1982

Summer

Our rented holiday cottage sits lightly on sand, from which harsh grasses stick up raggedly and prick our bare feet. Charlie, my grandson, who is two years old and hearty as the day is long, does not mind, but Mary, my daughter, and I watch where we put our feet. Our house fits us. White clapboard, with a screened porch, it has exactly the amount of space we need without an inch to spare. It is furnished with surprisingly comfortable, very ugly, cushioned bamboo couches and chairs. One small bookcase is filled with the owner's paperback books—romances with garish covers, touchingly tattered. Its heart is the sunny kitchen, which has cupboards full of all sorts of pots and pans ranging from immense kettles for cooking the corn we buy fresh from local farms to tins with little hollows Mary fills with delectable bran muffins stuffed with raisins. We revel in peaches and blueberries and tomatoes and lettuces and fat fresh peas. Every day is a pleasure.

I begin each day with a solitary early morning walk on the beach, during which I am often the only person in sight. I step on tide-washed sand and run my eye along the blue-gray eastern horizon between sea and sky. If I slice this line into segments, each appears to be straight, but the sweep of the whole curves to render the world perceptibly round. Just so, an individual life can appear to be isolated and without purpose unless recognized as contributing continuity to lives that precede it and follow it, endowing each human span with rich universality.

One year ago almost to this day I was in the air flying home from Australia, to which I traveled on a grant from the Australia Arts Council. I have measured the roundness of the earth, gloried in its character even as I endured its distances: a direct flight from Sydney to Los Angeles takes seventeen hours. But flying as a passenger does not test sinew and heart. I would have preferred to have traveled on a full-rigged American clipper ship in the nineteenth century, on the Great Circle route from Liverpool, England, by way of the South Atlantic, around Antarctica to Melbourne and back through the Falkland Islands. This voyage took sixty to eighty days and was then a marvel of speed; the route curved neatly around the earth and took advantage of the mighty winds of the Southern Hemisphere.

When I walk on the shore each morning, I like to paddle in the water and to think of its furious, relentless movement around the earth. To remember Sir Ernest Shackleton's landfall at King Haakon Sound on South Georgia Island in 1916:

Just east of us was a marvelous pile of driftwood, covering half an acre, and piled from four to eight feet high in places. This was a graveyard of ships—woeful flotsam and jetsam—sport of the sea: lower masts, topmasts, a great mainyard, ships' timbers, bones of brave ships, and bones of brave men. Most of it had drifted a thousand miles from Cape Horn, some of it two thousand miles or more.

Swept before the westerly gales on to this wild South Georgian coast, the easterly current, by some strange freak of eddies, threw it up in this one spot—a sad tale of wasted human endeavor, of gallant seamen beaten by the remorseless sea. Piled in utter confusion lay beautifully carved figureheads, well-turned teak stanchions with brass caps, handrails clothed in canvas "coachwhipping" finished off with "Turks' heads"—the proud work of some natty, clever AB; cabin doors, broken skylights, teak scuttles, binnacle stands, boats' skids, gratings, headboards, barricoes, oars, and "harness casks." There the mighty roaring Southern Ocean, tiring of its sport, had cast them up contemptuously to rot, in grievous memory of proud, tall ships with lofty spars, of swift clippers, barques, barquetines, possibly even an old East Indiaman. Wreckage from schooners, sealers, whalers, poachers, pirates, and maybe even bits of a man-o'-war, lay around, for some of it may even have drifted there when Drake first battled around the Horn. *

We dwell as strangers on the earth to become its wrack. We invent it for ourselves. We name it land and sea and sky. We divide its reaches arbitrarily into degrees of latitude and longitude, supplemented by a contrivance we call time. We keep ourselves in orderly fashion by imposing on it grids entirely our own. We forget, because we have

*F. A. Worsley, *Shackleton's Boat Journey* (New York: W. W. Norton and Company, 1977), pp. 182–183.

to in order to endure our plight, that these are rationales of our own logic. Colonists, we attune ourselves to it as we may—but we remain strangers. Indifferent to us, the earth rolls under our feet among other phenomena like itself.

I contemplate all this with curiosity and wonder, and then return to my daughter and grandson.

A white rattlesnake, pale as milk, has invaded my dreams. Night before last I encountered it rather casually, recognizing it instantly as too young (only about ten inches long, and slender) to be very harmful. I seized it behind its triangulated head, and somehow that was that.

Last night I grasped it as firmly, walked to the wide veranda of the elaborate sandalwood cage of a house I seem to be living in in these dreams, and set it free into the lush tangle of the insect-humming garden. But in the meander of my dream, the little snake kept reappearing. Twice as if it were a coiled carving above the lintel of a low door, and then simply materializing over and over in my path as I walked through empty, wide-windowed rooms. Once it bit me high on the ankle. I came to know that it intended to stay with *me,* personally.

Frightened (obviously such a young creature would grow and become dangerous) and irritated too (a nuisance in my establishment), I twice had a cage made for it; but I noticed without reproving him that the turbaned servant (I am in an Eastern land) had made the cages too largely meshed. I began to feel an impulse to accept the snake, as I had learned to accept the unknowable jungle surrounding my house, which too had its inconveniences and mysteries. In one of my attempts to get it to live outside in the garden, I examined it carefully, from a householder's viewpoint. Its eyes were a pale blue to match its milky skin, its scales white like the lining of a shell. Against my will, I felt a kinship with it. Young, it fell naturally into my care. But I was afraid, and even tried to squeeze it to death, pretending that I needed to hold it hard to keep it from biting me again. I was relieved as I came eventually to think I had banished it.

But the gardener, a venerable mute man, interrupted me one night as I sat reading placidly in a wide-winged woven chair on the veranda. He brought me a shallow china bowl full of vegetable soup, in which the little white snake lay curled, as if contented. The gardener gave me to understand that this soup is what the snake likes to eat and will grow best on; also that I must in duty provide this nourishing protection. Mistress in my own house, I calmly accepted, placed the bowl on a table beside my chair, and continued to read.

But I woke up feeling very frightened. Is the white snake my own death? Must I sustain my own death as naturally as my other responsibilities?

1 8   J U L Y

The Japanese say that "art is the palm of the hand; the arts are the fingers."* By analogy, the source of our vitality eludes us. We finger the world around us with our senses, which deliver it to us in an idiosyncratic formulation. Our bodies serve to introduce the world to us.

They also, as importantly, introduce us to other people, who can help us to understand who we are because we

*Faubion Bowers, *Japanese Theatre* (New York: Hermitage House, 1952).

7

never see ourselves. My sister Louise wrote in a recent letter:

Curious that you should mention your walks to and from junior high school, for I remember well your daily going back and forth, seeing you now, with your books strapped together, swinging around the screen in the dining room to go out through the kitchen door, your pigtails tied with stiff ribbons, bobbing on your shoulders. You were serious, solemn, a touch severe. In fact, the view of you I think is almost my earliest in-the-round memory of you. I say in-the-round because it was the first time I felt the presence of your separate personality. You marched around that screen and in your stride I could sense the independence you had. Further, I saw that you had a life of your own which interested you a lot and on which you were concentrating. Looking back now, the quality I most strongly felt was your concentration, sensing, quite accurately I think, that this was the avenue that led to your independence—and, of course, to your separation out from the family. I suppose what I was watching was the process of your essence emerging and placing you in the world, in relation to other people.

When I read this description, I recalled as vividly as if I were in that old self the swing I had made, and the determination I had felt. This kind of physical continuity sustains me as I age, and I can summon up when I need it the energy I had when I was young. The other day my grandson Charlie suddenly pelted toward the ocean while I was watching him for Mary. As I ran to catch him, I saw that he was churning along much faster than I had calculated, and for a terrible moment I realized that I was not going to be able to make it to him before he plowed into the waves. Then, as if released from a coiled spring, energy took charge of me: I ran faster than I think I have ever run in my life and as I ran I felt as if I were rising above the surface of the sand, scarcely touching it. Even in the exigency of my fear, the image of a Grecian figure, draperies afloat, flashed across my mind. I could have run forever, and I caught him easily by the hand to shepherd him playfully along the edge of the surf.

22 JULY

When I return in my imagination to my jungle-garden dreams—and they linger in my mind—I notice that the snake is filling out. Curled in the porcelain bowl, its pearlescent scales glisten with health.

Is it D. H. Lawrence's Mexican "plumed serpent"? Was my intense and instant terror of Mexico on my first trip there in 1950 with my then well-beloved husband, James, an adumbration of his violent, self-inflicted death there thirty-one years later? His death, on November 17, 1981, erupted into my life. Self-inflicted. The hand I had known so well and had loved so much, turned against the life I had cherished. And, even in the bleak separation of ten years of divorce, had continued to cherish. Twenty-four years of marriage do not disperse. I knew him, I felt, as I knew myself. Married when we were both twenty-six, we enjoyed, in the golden light of our youth, a world we made of one another in a communication so replete it seemed to need no words.

Marriage allowed me to harbor self-delusion, as if by placing my hand in James's I had delivered into it a range of experience that I would not have to learn for myself because he would at once develop knowledge of it and protect me from that knowledge. I could be one half of the whole we made together, I thought; I could choose "the good" and eschew "the evil."

So I lived to an extent protected from "sharp and sided hail" as surely as Gerard Manley Hopkins's nun in a refuge "out of the swing of the sea."* The realities of my work in art, of bringing up my children alone, of earning our living, rocked this magic protection, but beat in vain against its delicate translucent membrane. Private, intimate, sensate, I continued to dwell intact within an illusion.

Just as I had no idea that I was living by habit within this imagined protection, so I had no forewarning of James's death, though on that day I felt strangely sad. (I remember asking my graduate student assistant at the University of Maryland, where we were teaching a drawing class, why the light was leaving the sky; his look of surprise when he gazed at it and said all was as usual.) James's death was a fact as hard as a stone. I took it in first through my children, distanced it in them. By feeling their pain, I protected myself from my own. Months and months went by, day following day, in which a kind of mad normality held me numb. Until a February afternoon in 1982, three months after his death. I was quietly reading Antonia White's *The Lost Traveller*, when the twin of the white serpent who has recently joined me loomed up into my consciousness.

The protagonist of the book has for years debated whether or not to become a Catholic. During a church service, his eye falls idly on a woman, and *"Suddenly, without warning, the demons of his imagination leapt on her, stripping her, using her with a cold brutality of lust. He was not looking at her, but, as if she had guessed his thoughts, he felt her shift further away from him.*

"At that, his fever left him. His flesh turned cold; he was weighed down by an enormous oppression of guilt. For the first time in his

*Gerard Manley Hopkins, "Heaven-Haven."

10

life, he seemed to grasp the meaning of evil. He was conscious of something corrupt in the depths of his nature; something at once frigid, impure and violent . . . had a peculiar malignancy that tainted the very source of the spirit. He felt as if he were isolated from every human contact; locked in a dark cell that was both icy and suffocating." *

Into that cell I abruptly fell, so far down into a chasm of myself I had not even suspected existed that my terror was categorical, unqualified by what would normally be called feeling. And in the dense dark of the very bottom my hand came to temperatureless scales that stirred slightly at my touch: a reptile. As if I hoped to rise out of this cavern on cross-currents of trapped wind, my mind tried to rescue me by mocking the banality of the symbolism. I tried not to believe it but it remained brutally true. Evil was *alive.* All complacency fled, I knew without hope of return to inno-cence a malignancy in myself so unmistakable that I would forever more have to take it into consideration. A malig-nancy, furthermore, that had its own energy, was indepen-dent of me while at the same time somehow fitting me.

It is a good thing that life is so daily, for here in the sunny progression of my days with Mary and Charlie—our swims and our walks and our expeditions to vegetable and fruit stands in the countryside, our naps and our reading and our relish of one another's company—I am moved to be easy with my two serpents. During the last few days, the white snake has somehow grown to intertwine as an equal with its black-green twin. They are heraldic in my imagination now: Good and Evil—a medieval mandala.

My daughters' attitude toward marriage is altering my

*Antonia White, *The Lost Traveller,* a Virago Modern Classic (New York: Dial Press, 1950), pp. 22–23.

own, reenforcing the turn that James's death made in it. Alexandra, my older daughter, has a streak of robust realism that runs underneath all her adjustments. Mary has separated from her husband and courageously confronts her responsibilities. My daughters conceive of themselves as ground to be held, a stance that I have come to only reluctantly and over a long period of years.

Autumn

Summer is over and our family is scattered. Alexandra, her husband, and their two little sons are living in New York. Mary and Charlie are there too; Mary is studying at Hunter College toward a graduate degree in literature. My son, Sam, is at Kenyon College for his junior year. I am once again in my routine of telephone calls and letters. Surely one of the pleasures of parenthood is writing letters to grown-up children: details that would bore other people are received as nourishment, proof that their family ground is firm under their feet. The University of Maryland has begun its fall term. I teach in the art department two days a week; already the students' lives are counterpointing mine as I take in their ideas and their work.

I have come to appreciate the autonomy of living alone. The sun is shining on me as I write. A good sort of day for picking my figs and making jam. That will be a fine smell in this brisk air: figs and lemon chunks with a dash of ginger. My tomato plants cannot hold up all their bounty and must be pruned and tacked up on their supporting cages. Yellow and white chrysanthemums are blooming all over my garden, along with a riot of marigolds and zinnias.

6 SEPTEMBER

Before he left for New York, I began teaching Charlie to walk safely up and down the stairs of my house. At the top, I take his hand and say, "Slowly and carefully." He holds on and repeats, "Slowly and carefully," and we descend, one step at a time, watching our feet. On his own, he would step off into space, focusing on the middle distance. As I coached him down the other morning, I heard my nurse's voice instructing me in the same way, and remembered suddenly how rash and clumsy I was at Charlie's age. How often I had toppled because I had rushed ahead into just the middle distance he focuses on; how awkward I had felt and how difficult it had been to adjust the pulleys and levers of muscles so that I could move forward smoothly. Charlie is learning fast. As he approaches the stairs from either end, he reminds himself, "Slowly and carefully." And if he feels me in a hurry, he says prudently, "Slowly and carefully, Granny!"

His words stay with me. I am now learning from my grandchildren, even as I learn from my children. To go "slowly and carefully" is what I will need to do in the next few weeks. Pantheon Books publishes *Daybook* on October 12. Two days later, the Baltimore Museum of Art marks the opening of its new wing with a dinner and a concert. Among other exhibitions: Grace Hartigan, Morris Louis, Clyfford Still, Anne Truitt. On October 15, the museum is giving a dinner and a ball. On October 20, André Emmerich, my dealer in New York since 1963, will give a party at his gallery to celebrate the publication of *Daybook*. Alexandra and Mary are having a dinner after the party. When I was less experienced, I used to step off into such a sequence of events much as Charlie would like to do on the stairs—focusing on a middle distance and hoping for the best. Now I take forethought. But I remain naturally impulsive, and have to remember to be prudent.

18 SEPTEMBER

Daybook is printed. When I first held a copy in my hands, I felt a profound satisfaction. Not so much satisfaction with the writing, though I did my best and would not change a word, as with the quite ordinary feeling of having finished something, combined with pleasure in its physicality—the kind of completion I am accustomed to in my work in sculpture and painting.

My children like the book. Alexandra sent me masses of stately scarlet roses, which I will dry into potpourri in a pale jade green bowl that Mary gave me to celebrate. Sam telephoned to say that I must keep on writing every day.

22 SEPTEMBER

I continue to grieve for James. His suicide looms like a great scarped rock in a desert, pitted and fissured, cutting off the horizon of his life. Leading to this rampart, a path I do not know and cannot guess, though I have tried.

I wander through the early years of our marriage. As he was then he belongs entirely to me now, held beyond harm, come by death into my possession. Had I loved him inordinately, I could prune and cultivate my unique memory of him until he would be unrecognizable to himself—perhaps a not uncommon course in grief.

I wander in the early years of our marriage not so much by choice as because that is the way James comes into my mind. I seem to see him out of the corner of an eye, to catch glimpses. A spotlight of memory picks him out. He is standing by the ocean in a characteristic attitude of attention, his head slightly tilted; he wears white trousers and a white shirt with the sleeves rolled up over his brown, golden-haired arms; in his intelligent hands the inevitable books and magazines and papers. He is dressing for a dinner; he opens the left top drawer of his bureau, takes out a white linen handkerchief and tucks it into his dinner jacket pocket; he turns and looks at me quizzically: he is ready to go. He walks toward me up the aisle of a train; I smell the anachronistic dusty plush; he has on a blue and white striped seersucker suit; his smile broadens as he comes; he is enjoying walking toward his wife.

I am not healed. I am crying. Soft tears as devoid of bitterness as the rain now falling gently in the dark dawn.

I am not always so unbitter. He wantonly took with him the years he could have had with my children and their children. He squandered their faith in him and laid waste to what could have been, as they grew older, a whole territory.

I do not understand his suicide. Within the strictest of definitions, our lives are all that we possess. Their voluntary forfeit has been part of my thinking ever since childhood, when I began to read and to consider gratuitous heroism;

I can understand that. It is self-destruction as escape that seems to me wrongful because it usurps divine ordinance, by which death is sanctified. Also, I simply do not understand hopeless extremity. I have to acknowledge it without the help of empathy, and to fall back humbly on the principle of compassion.

The Francis Scott Key Book Shop in Georgetown, a part of Washington in which James and I lived for some years, gave me a book-signing party yesterday. Copious copies of *Daybook* were displayed in the front bay window to the right of the shop's narrow gray wooden doors, through which we used often to pass in the early days of our marriage. Perhaps it may have crossed James's mind then that he might one day see a book of his there (I wish he had), but never once did it cross mine that I would see one of my own.

I have been taken by surprise by the recent events of my life, but this can only be because I have not been alert to the signs that in retrospect intimate their direction. If I could tune in now, the future would be as legible as the past. An unassuming gratification underlies the layers of my feelings about what is happening to me. My life has accumulated behind my own back while I was living it, like money in the bank, and I am receiving its accruement.

Alexandra came down from New York for the book-signing party, and for the lovely, friendly dinner that followed it. It is a joy to wake up and know that she is under my roof, to take her breakfast in bed, to listen to her speak of her life, and to shelter her under my wing. She is tired, as the mothers of little children are usually tired; Sammy is three years old, Alastair one year. I always feel a unique ease when I am alone with one of my children. It is as if we both return gratefully to a condition of mutuality. This is a special pleasure now that they are grown up, as the mutuality that was once exclusive is enhanced by the ongoing history of our lives together.

I 2   O C T O B E R

Daybook is published today.

It will not be reviewed in *The New York Times Book Review*, I am told. I feel taken aback, as the current books I know are usually reviewed there and this exclusion seems to me to turn *Daybook* into a nonbook. But I am old in the ways of rejection and failure. Sturdy in the common sense that recognizes maverick forces, resolute in my faith in the work I do as honestly as I can, I am supported by the rationale of my experience.

But publishing a book is strange to me, so unlike the reverberative opening of an art exhibit when artists stand in full public view beside their work. I am alone here in my house. It is a perfectly ordinary day, during which I have to do nothing at all. In fact, I *can* do nothing. I wonder whether the publication of this book is going to change my life as little as an exhibit usually does when after the opening I simply return once again to my studio to confront the constrictions with which the course of any life is beset.

I 5   O C T O B E R

The new wing of the Baltimore Museum of Art opened last night. When I entered the gallery in which my sculptures are installed, I fell back—actually stepped back—before the force of my own feelings distilled into forms rendering visible their own beings. Tears rose to my eyes and from that freshet of feeling the unchangeable and unchanging truth: I am always, and always will be, vulnerable to my own work, because by making visible what is most intimate to me I endow it with the objectivity that forces me to see it with utter, distinct clarity. A strange fate. I make a home for myself in my work, yet when I enter that home I know how flimsy a shelter I have wrought for my spirit. My vulnerability to my own life is irrefutable. Nor do I wish it to be otherwise, as vulnerability is a guardian of integrity.

The world can make no meet response to art. Praise can miss the point as much as a casual remark such as I overheard last night: an impeccably turned-out gentleman bounding up the stairs to the gallery exclaimed over his shoulder, "And now to see the minimalist—or maximalist!" He had all the relish of a casually greedy person with a tasty tidbit in view; he was on his way to gulp down my life with as little consideration as he would an artichoke heart.

Do I wish, can I afford, in my own limitations, to continue to make work that has such a high psychic cost and stands in jeopardy of being so met? Do I have a choice? I do not know. Neither whether I can further endure, nor whether I can stop. The work is preemptory. My life has led me to an impasse.

Paintings by Morris Louis, whom I knew only slightly but with whom I feel akin, hung on the walls of the gallery adjacent to mine. Awash in the murmur of the usual art talk, I regarded them as I might look to trusted comrades for support. Looking at the Clyfford Stills, I understood, for the first time, why he immured himself in a tiny Maryland town as fortress; why he used suddenly to take off on cross-continental drives alone—his equivalent of my solitary walks. In the course of wandering the museum until I could decently leave, I confronted a Cézanne and felt as if a muscular hand had taken mine and Cézanne stood beside me, grubby with clotted paint, silent in his own life, impelled by its force to record it.

While it is not true that only artists understand art, for there are in every generation some people who not only understand it but also enhance its reach by appreciation, there is a freemasonry among us. We stand shoulder to shoulder, generation to generation.

10 NOVEMBER

Two facts differentiate *Daybook* from my work in visual art.

The first is the simple safety of numbers. I am accustomed to one long effort producing one object. There are 6500 *Daybook*s in the world. My contribution to them was entirely mental, emotional. I never put my hand on a single one of these objects until I picked up a printed book. I made no physical effort; no blood, no bone marrow moved from me to them. I do not mean that I made no effort. On the contrary, the effort was excruciating because it was so without physical involvement, so entirely hard-wrought out of nothing physical at all; no matter how little of the material world goes into visual art, *something* of it always does, and that something keeps you company as you work. There seems to me no essential difference in psychic cost between visual and literary effort. The difference is in what emerges as result. A work of visual art is painfully liable to accident; months of concentration can be destroyed by a careless shove. Not so 6500 objects. This fact gives me a feeling of security like that of living in a large, flourishing, and prosperous family.

Ancillary to this aspect is the commonplaceness of a book.

People do not have to go much out of their way to get hold of it, and they can carry it around with them and mark it up, and even drop it in a tub while reading in a bath. It is a relief to have my work an ordinary part of life, released from the sacrosanct precincts of galleries and museums. A book is also cheap. Its cost is roughly equivalent to its material value as an object, per se. This seems to me more healthy than the price of art, which bears no relation to its quality and fluctuates in the marketplace in ways that leave it open to exploitation. An artist who sells widely has only to mark a piece of paper for it to become worth an amount way out of proportion to its original cost. This aspect of art has always bothered me, and is one reason why I like teaching: an artist can exchange knowledge and experience for money in an economy as honest as that of a bricklayer.

The second fact differentiating *Daybook* is that in it I am speaking English, a legible language. What I have said in it is being more understood than misunderstood. By contrast, I realize now how few people can read meaning in the visual syntax of art.

The letters that I am receiving from my readers surprise me, and touch me deeply. When I decided in 1974 to record my life with the hope that I would learn from what I wrote, I felt a dumb faith in the simple act of honest witness. I am seeing that faith extrapolated into a larger field within which honesty is answered by equal honesty. A direct line lies open between an author and readers, and along it feeling flows in both directions. I answer each letter with care, and with gratitude. The word "love" is much abused, but there is a kind of love in this communication.

James died one year ago today. The last time I saw him was some years ago when, one sunny summer afternoon, Alexandra and Mary brought him for tea. I made oatmeal cookies and wore a cool blue and white flowered cotton dress and my single strand of Japanese pearls. After tea, after conversation with an old mutual friend and the girls, reminiscent of many such conversations in our lifetime together —James witty and the ladies laughing—our friend departed and Alexandra and Mary took themselves off for a short visit next door. James politely asked to see my studio. We walked out into my garden and he said neutrally nice things about my plants. He stood in the studio, flooded with sun and the colors of my legions of glass paint jars, and said with wistful honesty, "You are so organized." We returned to the living room, I to my white rocking chair and he to a little straight armchair we had inherited from his father. We had nothing more to say. He had remarried. I had been as polite about his new wife as he about my garden. Then, in the sudden silence, we happened to turn toward each other at the same second and looked straight into one another's eyes. For an immeasurable moment, nothing separated us. I took in the extraordinary fact that in that instant we had ceased to be two people but were, as if enchanted, one, impersonal and timeless; then two again—abashed, but somehow *all right.* We made a little desultory conversation. The girls returned, we moved to the front porch. I stood on tiptoe and lightly kissed his cheek good-bye.

I have not made any new sculptures for one year. Sheets of color flood my inner eye, but no work presents itself, whole.

Winter

These are sober days. I depart from the art building at the university into luminist sunsets, splendid mists graced by long thin clouds horizontal to a reflective earth, but by the time I get home it is pitch dark. A dearly loved friend died a few weeks ago, taking with her forever a sweet companionship that has gladdened my life for thirty-five years; and her counsel, always sound, wise, affectionate, and apt. The space in which my memories dwell is shrinking to what I am forced to remember alone. On the face of another friend just as beloved, an ashen shadow underlies the contraction with which the flesh shrinks from death. His eyes avoid mine. We keep our voices cheerful but neither of us mentions a future we tacitly fear we are not going to share.

The other evening while I was walking to a tea in Georgetown through a sleety rain, I paused idly to watch through the slats of a venetian blind a maid preparing dinner. She worked in a familiar kind of house; beyond her a door obviously led to a dining room with a bay window overlooking a formal garden—a room for all seasons, I thought: Christmas, Easter; birthdays, weddings, funerals; Father, Mother, children, grandchildren, sisters and brothers, aunts, uncles, cousins, friends. Outside, on the icy street, I watched the deliberate, accustomed movements of the maid and thought of the days when I myself lived in a house like this, and used to walk into just such a kitchen, just such a dining room, mistress of the house. As I turned away to walk on, I glanced down at my feet on the glistening bricks. I felt under my soles the unevennesses of tree roots pushing up against their patterned order. Just like the brick pavements of my childhood, I thought, and stretched my toes happily. I am at home on this wet pavement. I like being alone, looking, musing, walking on when I choose. The life I have suits me as my childhood suited me. Much, much more than running any such household anywhere with anyone. An echo of my father's voice reading Kipling followed me down the dark street: ". . . the Cat that walks by himself, and all places are alike to him."

19 DECEMBER

It hit me early today that I am not going to be able to die as I would like to—cleanly. Too many vital channels attach me to the people I love, as well as to certain habits of mind and body, to desires unlikely to be fulfilled and desires I am trying to fulfill. I was turning this situation over in my mind when I suddenly caught a glimpse of myself in the oval mirror of my bureau: slightly bent head, still body, against my freshly starched white embroidered curtains. "There is no solution," I thought, even as I realized that the body I was looking at was worn, its years numbered. It seemed to me that for the first time in my life I had finally reached an end to what I could accomplish by my own effort.

An end as real as that of my childhood when I used to stand on the marshy banks of the Eastern Shore of Maryland and face into the tidal waters. I remember my frustration when it became clear that I could only walk back and forth along the shore; I could not advance into the river and could only imagine what the view would be like from there. In the same way, I cannot imagine death. I must tread my tracks. It then occurred to me that dying might be not so much *leaving* these tracks, now over the years become cherished, as continuing along them into some entirely new territory. I have all my life moved on without undue fuss when the need to move became more compelling than the need to stay. I can hope that the step onto the path of death may, when I actually get to it, be as natural.

I can hope, but I must also work, I think, on detaching myself from the very accumulation of my life which is now bringing to me results that are strengthening me. The publication of *Daybook* has changed my life, tying me by myriad tiny threads to its readers, known and unknown. When I was a child, I had to take a nap every afternoon and used to read surreptitiously the books exiled to the children's floor of our house in Easton, Maryland. One of these was a large edition, beautifully illustrated, of Swift's *Gulliver's Travels.* The text was in French, which I could not read, but I pored over the pictures, most often over the one in which

Gulliver is tied down by the six-inch-high Lilliputians while he is asleep: there lay the immense Gulliver rendered helpless by countless tiny lines pegged to the ground. Even the hairs on his head were anchored. So it is that every work of my life attaches me to that life. In this situation, death would be a bloody business.

The irony is that I have worked hard to make each of these attachments. I have a stockpile of sculptures, paintings, and drawings—every work of art I have made that has not sold—in a storage space for which I pay every month as regularly as I pay my utility bills. This is a sensible arrangement, as I can leave this work to my children. Most of the time I never give it a thought, but this morning it flashed across my mind that if it were blown away I would be bereaved in a way that would hurt me very much. I have not been inordinately materialistic, but I am attached to my house, to my inherited belongings, and to the things that I have chosen for myself. All these objects add complexity to my emotional ties to the people with whom I have shared, and share, my life, and to my aspirations for myself.

For some twenty years now I have begun each day with a period of quiet. During this time, I experience a state of mind in which I am to a degree detached from my daily life. I like this feeling, and it occurs to me that I have even begun to prefer it. If a dollar is offered to a person clutching a penny, the penny can be dropped without privation.

21 DECEMBER

At three yesterday afternoon Sam telephoned to say that his car had broken down on his way home from his college in Ohio and he was stranded, with just a few dollars, in Frostburg, Maryland, about 130 miles away. Without giving it much thought, I said I would drive right over and pick him up. I ate a little something and set out, accustomed to driving long distances easily. Within an hour the light began to fade. I drove faster and faster. Ice began to form on the road. I had to slow down, and then had to slow even more as the road became steeper, curving up and up in the Appalachian Mountains toward the Cumberland Gap. Full night descended. Very few cars were on the icy road. I felt more and more tired, and very much more frightened than I had been for years: advancing into darkness and ice, into a landscape that closed down over the road—huge, vague mountains looming on either side, steeper and steeper. Fewer and fewer cars; often I was alone. Snow began to fall. And, for the first time in my adult life, I began to panic. My hands trembled on the wheel. At the bottom of a ravine, I saw a light: a filling station. I pulled in. A primitive little place: one very young man in blue jeans, casual as the young seem more and more as I age; an outside telephone booth in the semidark, blown by snow. I telephoned the hotel in Frostburg where Sam was supposed to be. By this time I had utterly lost my usual feeling of competence. Even my voice was trembling. A man answered. Laughter in the background. Yes, there was a young man with glasses. Sam's voice was like the voice of God. He was fine. He would get a taxi. Where was the filling station? I asked the casual youth, who by this time had begun to grasp my fearful state and came out into the snow to the telephone to give Sam directions. I was to wait, Sam said. He would be there in about half an hour. "Don't worry, Mom."

Clutching my bright blue woolen scarf to my throat, I waited. Drank two cups of very hot coffee, ate some peanut butter crackers. Talked with a series of harsh-hewn country men who appeared and disappeared. The youth allowed as how he had to close the filling station in fifteen minutes. Headlights rounded down off the mountain out of a snowy cloud: Sam—calm, efficient, familiar. He drove us competently back home.

But harm has been done. I have come face to face with age itself. Inelasticity. An unrelenting wall of physical weakness that no amount of willpower dented: I *could not* have done more. And no spring of energy rose in me as it did only five months ago when I caught Charlie at the beach. I am not exactly ashamed. That would be silly. I am changed. Irreversibly changed.

1983

I am trying to feel out the new topology that the publication of *Daybook* is drawing around me: enlarging dimensions with amoeboid edges sensitive to changing forces outside and inside myself; but I seem also to have developed *up*. To have become more visible, as if I were a hill that had swelled into prominence from some inner accrual of substance. What I must in honesty name achievement in the real sense of actualized potentiality has made a topographical change. The hill of my prominence is modest, in due proportion to the plain from which it has risen. Still, I am having to accustom myself to being visible instead of indistinguishable in a stretch of land.

But I have made no new sculpture since 18 November 1981, when Alexandra appeared at my door to tell me of her father's death the night before. Inert, dumb, numb; when stirred, stirred only by a vagrant air into which I have turned in vain my blind face.

I was only sluggishly pleased when a student told me recently that she had made her way in a sad and bewildered state of mind to the place where my work stands in the Corcoran Gallery of Art, and had felt when she saw it as if she had "come home." It is validating that she feels my work, as I do, to be a kind of home, but she seemed to me to be talking of a dead artist.

Another death in a series of deaths, for the shrunken look I saw on my old friend's face last month was a true omen: he is dying. Dying to me, but not necessarily to himself— that is important to remember, but cold comfort to set against his loss.

2 2 J A N U A R Y

It is paradoxical that even in this heaviness I feel unusually free and easy, and it occurred to me suddenly the other night when I was driving myself home from a dinner that this may be because I am not in love with anyone. I feel independent, as I did when I was a child, before I came to understand the promise and responsibility of gender. As soon as this concept became clear to me—at about the age of nine when Mother read me *Jane Eyre*—I began to predispose myself toward union with a man whom I would love and by whom I would be beloved.

Very little reality reined my imagination. My father was not even a tiny bit romantic: shorter than my mother, indecisive; chatty, entertaining but in no way a romantic hero. I had no inkling then of the blessing such a gift for intimacy as his can be, for he was an easy and comfortable man to be with and I owe to him the pattern of the many platonic friendships that have graced my life. I had no brothers to scuff me up, to tease and tumble me. By the time I left my governess's maiden hands for the fifth grade of a public school, my romantic ideals were so embellished and so alluring to me that I simply discounted whatever I saw in the boys around me and looked forward happily to one day encountering and succumbing to a gentle, powerful, and mysterious man who would recognize me as cataclysmically as I would him. We would embrace, and remain together all our lives, which would end at the same moment in a sort of transfiguration into a radiant painted cloud.

So I dreamed up this man, cherished him in my imagination, and gradually grew dependent on him. It was the image of this phantom lover that I projected onto James. It had to do not so much with a pattern of relationship (I was too ignorant to think pragmatically) as with a feeling of light. A radiance at once dim, so that it successfully hid those parts of James which he wished to keep to himself and which I had not the experience even to guess existed, and glorious. He shone for me as pure as gold.

It was this glow that his brutal death struck dark. So it is no wonder that for over a year I have been like a lake of ice under a pale sky. Up to the second of his death—despite the history of our lives together, our separation, and his remarriage, and even the meeting in which we found that we had nothing to say to one another—he had been irradiated by this romantic ray. The image in my mind had clamped over him when I fell in love with him, and had stuck to him. I could never pull it off by will, reason, desperation, or prayer. Relieved by his death of my stubborn girlish dreams, I am given back to myself, enriched by years of thoroughly lived experience and released into command of that experience.

The intimation of my own weakening toward death that
made such a sharp turn in my life during my drive last
December to Cumberland Gap has lingered with me, partly
in the form of fascination with parts of the world I am now
almost inevitably not going to see. And animals I am not
going to encounter, like the snow leopard who lives in the
higher reaches of the Himalayas. In George Schaller's photograph of one such leopard, she leaps into focus.* Her
neat-eared head tilts forward from her humped shoulders
and her broad forelegs, each so powerful that together they
outspan the breadth of her massive oval jaw. Her pelage is
three colors: gray white and orange tan splashed with
umber spots like hypnotic blossoms. Her body is so elu-
sively absorbed into the snow and rocks echoing her pattern
that I at first took her tail to be an oddly shaped rock until
I saw how its acute angle matched the startling intelligence
of her gaze. I loved her on sight, a strange strong cat stalk-
ing high lands I shall never visit. She will lay her bones on
the earth as I shall in time lay mine, land-wrack to match the
sea-wrack of King Haakon Sound.

I have been making awkward drawings on my dining room
table. I tell myself that I am reluctant to spend the money
to heat the studio but the truth is that I am afraid to take that
big a step and I need the companionship of my plants, which
I have gathered around me here in the sun. I lean over the
table, like a child who after a fright has retreated to her

*George B. Schaller, *Stones of Silence: Journeys in the Himalaya* (New York:
Viking, 1979).

nursery and her Mother Goose. I have made drawing after drawing after drawing. Yesterday, just under the wing of twilight, I drew two lines and added seven strokes of paint; I straightened up to look, and saw one of *my* drawings, identifiable. But it is only one.

The other morning while driving the bleak route to the university, it suddenly occurred to me that when I was married I had actually *eaten food earned by someone else.* I tasted something slimy and rotten in my mouth and felt a kind of servitude utterly familiar. With the force of a blow to the solar plexus, I felt clearly the position I had placed myself in: I had been beholden to James for the food in my mouth; I had been frightened that he would not put it there or in the mouths of my children; I had felt as if I owed him something because he kept me and the children—and that's the truth, I had owed him. As I took in these facts, the present fell into place around me in the most satisfactory way. I would much rather put on my stout oxfords and go out into the cold dark morning to earn my bread than take it from someone else. As I made the turn toward the campus, one among others of my own kind, earners, I actually shuddered with surprise that I ever could have lived off another person.

Then a second insight, like a second wave, swept over me: a recollection too profound to be named, of my blood moving through the unborn I had carried, and the riptide of their departure from the cavity of my body. And beyond that a further wave: to my horrified surprise—as my children are dearer to me than my blood—a wave of rage and anger, of outrage, at having been violated, invaded. The outrage of penetration and occupation. None of these feelings had ever been conscious before. I continued to drive smoothly as they swept over me and away from me, leaving me quivering with the same kind of awe I used to feel when a baby quickened in my womb: respect for the movement of an unknown being. In this case myself, rearing out of my own depths.

These days little things make me cry a little. The leaves of my plants glossy in the sun against the brilliant snow. Tiny oranges now fattening on my orange tree; amaryllis improbably jutting forth out of long stalks, heavy, bell-shaped scarlet blossoms; the furled buds of gardenias, and the finicky primrose that likes to be moved in and out of the sun so that sometimes its stout, rather coarse leaves and stiff vivid flowers stand out bravely, and sometimes lurk under the foliage of other plants that dapple them with shade. It is not sentimentality that plants respond to sensitive care; they just do. So I move among them, spraying here and touching there, and as I do I feel touched back.

Or I will be suddenly struck by the lively stillness of my living room, by the existence of an order dependent on my hand's care, coterminal with my life.

It is the deaths of my old friends that is raising the water table of my vulnerability. Of one particularly intimate group of vigorous and entertaining friends there are now so many dead. I am, save for one now dying, the only survivor. I live among their ghosts, but such is the power of my friends' liveliness in my imagination that it is a little as if *they* were living and *I* were the ghost. This is to an extent true, as the young woman (I can see me now: such smooth skin and shining yellow hair, awkward with eagerness, dignified by earnestness) who developed mental agility in the quick give-and-take converse of these animated friends is indeed gone. And, if I live long enough, I will be the only one who remembers her.

The fact of vitality remains vivid after death. Even more vivid than in life, as if death set this fact apart. Suspended in their death, my friends still live. But have left me here alone in the web we all took such delight in weaving.

Spring

How but in custom and in ceremony
Are innocence and beauty born?

—WILLIAM BUTLER YEATS

Here in this modest town of Easton on the Eastern Shore of Maryland, I grew up "in custom and in ceremony," daughter of its eighteenth-century ways. Looking back over the years that have brought me to this day of my sixty-second birthday, I feel more acutely than ever before how tenderly my parents sought to endow me with innocence and beauty. As I walk on the streets of my childhood, accompanied by my tall son, I ponder the tale of my life: a drama in which I had thought to cast myself as protagonist but have come over the years to assign myself a part as bit player, more moved than mover.

Sam and I are staying at the Tidewater Inn, which stands on the site of the burned-down Avon Hotel I remember so well: yellow and white clapboard surrounded by wide verandas on which dark green wicker rockers seemed never to stop rocking. When I turned on the water to wash my hands, I thought, "The same water . . ." as if I were refreshing myself at the spring tapped by the baby, the child, and the girl I once was here.

My life has not been what my parents envisioned. Even by the time I was four or five and began to walk around Easton on my short, strong legs and look at everything for myself, I had outgrown the white embroidered dresses they may have hoped would bind me to a life of innocence and beauty. I took to cotton gingham, to an independence in that context willful, and in so doing began to outgrow their custom and ceremony.

Nevertheless, I gratefully breathe their air here in this town of my childhood. Last night Sam and I walked around after dinner. I listened to him talk about Goethe's dictum that "Contradiction is the great begetter," and watched his head, towering over me, against the stars. I was tired, and stumbled, and realized as Sam gently caught my arm that the physical line of my resolute independence is running out in a long, slow turn.

WASHINGTON, D.C.

As I stood on the Oxford ferry yesterday, bracing myself against the wind and the waves, I realized that balance, not stability, is security. The channel was rough. I gripped a pocked green stanchion with one hand and held my long woolen scarf around my throat with the other; my feet delicately adjusted my weight to the crests of the waves. Color tinged the water down to the furthest reach of my eye: the water *is* color.

2 3   M A R C H

In the Shenandoah Valley, gray-blue limestone rocks emerge in lines like stilled waves from the grassy slopes, now spring green. Cows have calved. I was surprised the other day to see so many, mostly umber, a few black-and-white, and to see them so lively: two were running hard toward a herd. I have always thought of cows as sedentary, but as I watched that race I had a pang of empathy: born spirited, they soon grow into heavy barrels on brittle legs. Running must stop; their placid mien may be hard-won, a resignation to nature. The sheep have not yet lambed. Curlicued and plump, they seemed all to have their heads down to the new grass. Grass freshened by the showers of rain through which I drove, creeping one minute through a blinding torrent, cresting a hill a few minutes later into sunshine of that special radiance that breaks through clouds. In this broad valley, bounded on the west by the Allegheny Mountains, on the east by the Blue Ridge, the Shenandoah River runs smooth and shining as a river in a dream. Houses lie sweetly on the spines of the hills. Barns are eloquent of harvest. A valley for human habitation.

"Et in Arcadia ego. . . ." Even in the Shenandoah Valley lambs' births will drench the spring grass red with blood. In a few weeks that grass itself will lose its tenderness, and will prickle a bare foot. Out of the rounded, furry, playful calves: steaming, bitter yellow streams of urine; and they leave behind them, here and there on the graceful light gray rock waves and the emerald grass, dark brown corrugated fecal circles. They are from the moment of conception on their way to the butcher.

2 5   M A R C H

Walking around this morning to fetch a wrapper, brush my teeth, feed my cat, Jackson, make coffee, I heard my feet and recognized my father's quick trot. In the middle of last night I woke up and saw *Knot.* I have turned up the studio thermostat and will begin to work on it today. *Knot* is as clear as any sculpture I have ever seen in my life.

Yesterday a tornado ripped through that lovely part of my life in which I had thought Alexandra dwelt secure with her husband and children. Separation has struck them apart.

Tact is a subtle form of affection useful to the parents of married children. I have perhaps too deliberately refrained from speculation about her marriage in my attempt to reenforce it with respect. But the past is obsolete now. Alexandra spoke calmly when she told me, but the resolution in her voice chilled my blood; she watched me separate from her father, and could be in no doubt about the painful course that lies ahead of her. Her sons are with her; her husband has moved out of their apartment, as he must move out of my life, and I am sad for myself too: he was my first son-in-law and with careful kindness taught me how to be a mother-in-law. My heart turns in my body when I think of my grandsons; I have seen how poignantly his parents' separation rent Charlie's loyalties.

But it is Alexandra's pain that I feel most acutely. Once, back in the days that even so soon seem past recall, while she and Sammy, then two years old, were visiting me, he fell down the garden steps. I was standing by him when he suddenly toppled over backward, head first. I was able to catch him and break his fall, but in the second before I grasped his ankle the scenario of his broken neck ran through my mind along with the sight of his mother, just visibly pregnant, rushing toward us. As I consigned Sammy to possible instant death, the words "Alexandra will suffer" flashed across my mind, and I knew in that instant that the love of a parent for a child overwhelms all other ties.

I fell to sleep last night sick at heart, to wake up with *Knot* clear in my inner eye. I can only think that this unexpected wave of sorrow so tipped a fulcrum in my spirit that a balance shifted. I turned to *withstand,* as if in order to preserve my health, as a matter of life over death, and in so doing mysteriously put myself back in touch with the source of my work.

2 6   M A R C H

Two sculptures, *Knot* and another called *Amur,* are well started, and two paintings too. Yesterday was a normal day. A morning of work, lunch, a nap, more work. In the late afternoon, I cleaned the house rapidly, baked some oatmeal cookies, filled vases with forsythia and jonquils from my garden. Sat at my dinner table in candlelight with three old friends. I hear the steady hum of my inner gyroscope with inexpressible relief, and feel as if I had returned home after a long, dark, difficult journey to find my house alight.

This morning a thin mist permeates the peach-colored blur of budding trees. Under the glorious forsythia, spikes of iris beside a columbine. My day lilies need transplanting; they always spread unevenly as if to offset with crankiness their reliability. Last year's birthday primrose has settled into place near next fall's chrysanthemums. The fig tree, released from its winter fence of staked burlap, is already tipped with green. The climbing rose on the studio looks more graceful than it will again this year as it must straggle in order to bloom. Grape hyacinth and scilla are *pointilliste* spots of purest blue. I walked around sipping coffee from my Japanese cup, smelling and smiling and planning. But I would only have been passing the time had I not begun the day with a half hour of work in the studio.

My office at the University of Maryland is a small mezzanine room lit by a floor-length window overlooking the pit of a large drawing classroom with a clerestory through which I receive at second hand some natural light. I use a desk lamp instead of the merciless overhead fluorescent fixture. A steel desk, steel filing case, steel bookcase; orange plastic chairs. Two posters face me as I sit at my desk: a medieval tapestry depicting a heraldic maiden receiving in her lap the homage of a unicorn amid the flowers of innocence; Hadrian's handsome head, austere white marble against pure black. Behind my back, a sun-flooded Monet landscape and two postcard exhibition announcements: Alexander the Great and the American Luminists.

The only other office, and that more a laboratory than an

office, I have ever had was at Massachusetts General Hospital when I was a psychologist in my early twenties. There, too, I sat behind a desk, in authority and a starched white lab coat. Now, forty years later, the authority remains. I felt it on an afternoon last week when a student long graduated returned to talk over her life with me and, all of a sudden, while I was quietly listening, my Massachusetts General office imprinted itself over the scene like a photographic overlay: a dividing desk, a person speaking in troubled tones, and me sitting with hands folded on my lap. But the white coat has gone and with it the persona I discarded when I left the hospital: a cardboard placard of rectitude.

The hallmark of the change in me was empathy with the woman opposite. As she spoke, the range of my experience became accessible to me so that I could make it appropriately available to her.

She told me what was troubling her and so in the course of our discussion we came to speak of the abuses of guilt. Of the lag that sometimes exists, even for years, between an act and a realization that the act was wrong; of the surprise that realization can be, of the agonizing prick of compunction, the bite of remorse; and of how the habit of gnawing at oneself can lead to inanition so that addiction to one's own pain can block growth. We came finally to the purpose of repentance: the decision to learn from one's past in order to amend one's future.

When I was at Massachusetts General Hospital I did not understand compunction in any depth: in the idealistic flush of my early adulthood my misdeeds called attention to themselves and could be handled, often even rectified, with reasonable dispatch. In my late twenties and early thirties, I incurred the moral responsibilities I have lived out ever since. Some were in line with the stronger parts of my character, some with the weaker. All were in the strictest sense willful: they arose naturally, sometimes subtly, but all came sooner or later under the aegis of my will. I do not repudiate any of my actions—that would be to disown my life as well as to deprive myself of what my life has taught me—but, in common with all human beings, I have come over the years to recognize my failures to meet the standards I had hoped in my youth always to uphold. My conscience developed slowly, against the grain of impulse and of the rationalizations with which I artfully masked those parts of my behavior in which I wanted to persist without the ratchet of self-examination.

I try to consider my mistakes with the tenderness I would bring to bear on those of other people. In doing so, I notice that understanding leads to tempered self-forgiveness because my motivation, shorn of the incidental, seems to have constituted self-preservation. I have come to this position slowly, and with a lot of careful thought, because my instinctive reaction to any failure to meet my own standards is to blame myself mercilessly. Certain failures have been more useful than others in this change. One of these was a winter evening when I turned a grieving woman out of my house.

She was a stranger, a relative of a friend who had asked me to invite her for tea because she had recently suffered a terrible loss: her husband had been swept to his death in the Pacific Ocean while fishing. She had come to Washington in an attempt to offset her bereavement with a change of scene. It was a cold November evening. I lit a comforting fire and set myself to be hospitable. I had to set myself because I was not recovered from Sam's difficult birth a few weeks before and because James was drinking heavily. While my guest and I talked, I never lost sight of the fact that my husband lay upstairs in a deep depression and that I had to nurse my baby. As the time approached when I knew that I should in kindness invite her to stay for dinner,

I began to realize sadly that I must decide between her and myself: I did not have the leeway to be generous.

When she finally said that she had to go, I rose to my feet, called her a cab, and saw her out into the night. I have never forgotten the look she cast over her shoulder as she departed: despair barely masked in helpless acquiescence to convention. For I had used convention as a weapon and had hurt her—and myself—because I had hardened my heart and robbed it of sensitivity. Pride complicated my decision. Had I not wished to appear in control of my own life, I would have been able to explain my situation to her in such a way as to let her into it without burdening her with it. I need not have said what illness my husband had. I could have brought Sam down to the fire, nursed him there, let her hold him if she wanted to (a baby is comforting), and then given her dinner as I had given her trust. We would have met as two people in mutual understanding, and in mutual solace too.

One of the twelve labors Eurystheus demanded of Heracles was the cleansing of the Augean stables. King Augeus owned three thousand oxen; their stables had not been cleaned for thirty years; Heracles was ordered to clean them in one day. He diverted the Peneus and the Alpheus rivers so that they flooded the stables. I loved this story as a child, and used to picture the whole scene in brilliant sunlight: two broad bright blue sparkling rivers, wind-roughened into whitecaps as they rushed through an immense, wide-eaved wooden structure. A metaphor for repentance. Changing your behavior demands ingenuity, some cleverness in handling habitual patterns. A kind of psychological *jujitsu* comes into play to turn the strength of an attitude against itself so that a new attitude can be substituted. If repentance is genuine, it creates energy: there are always rivers to divert. And by bringing to bear on it entirely new forces, repentance makes permanent alterations in the landscape of a character, as well as in its emotional atmosphere. Heracles was a god. We humans are slower.

3 1   M A R C H

Alexandra and I have been talking over her separation from her husband. We are both at pains that she not feel any more bitter than she has to. Nor hold on to bitterness any longer than she needs in order to understand it within the largest possible context: that of our common human fallibility. For we are all in the grip of the unpredictable results of our actions, and nowhere is this unpredictability more clearly exposed than in divorce. And nowhere are the incitements to bitterness more intimate.

3   A P R I L

Last night blustery showers cleared the sky for a lemon dawn to shine this morning above clouds so opaque a gray that they appear to be a distant range of mountains. The earth is now pungent with spring, as if it were breathing.

Mary and Charlie are here for a visit. Charlie is almost three now and in his companionship I understand for the first time why people are attracted to the study of children in the abstract. He likes to dump my round red button box out onto the floor and pick over the buttons. He brings me two, three, four of a kind, or special ones that catch his eye —and my heart: shards of memory. He picks out details in daily life the same way. When he has matched them so that they make sense, he is gleeful. These cross-references become blocks of experience. He then juxtaposes them to make new cross-references, and suddenly we are conversing in a common context. I can ask questions and find out what he is thinking and feeling. I suppose I did this also with my own children but I cannot remember being as interested as I am now in the particulars of this unfolding development.

He relishes stories and this morning, in that delicious interval between a child's waking and hitting the ground for the day, Mary cuddled him in my bedroom armchair and regaled him with the tale of "The Three Little Pigs." I have always hated the end—so unfair to the Big Bad Wolf, who only wanted a meal. In Mary's revision the little pigs, safe in the third brother's stout brick house, turn the table: huff and puff such a wind up the chimney that the Big Bad Wolf is blown all the way back to his own front doorstep, where his mother is waiting for him and remarks comfortably, "Well, that's all right you couldn't catch a pig for supper. We'll have peanut butter and jelly sandwiches."

9 APRIL

Alexandra's separation from her husband has been such a shock that I am finding it difficult to adjust to it. I feel it mostly, of course, by way of the emotional reverberations it has set up within us all, particularly acute as they echo those we felt when Mary's marriage came to an end. But I also think of it as yet another anthropological change in what I have known of family life.

I was born into a triangulated family: two monoliths—Father and Mother—and me. I became bulkier and began to move about. My twin sisters, born eighteen months after me, added two more members, so we were Father, Mother, one oldest daughter, twin daughters: one male, four females. Father and Mother slowly but very surely (I watched) became less and less monolithic. When we were all about the same size, three of us split off, I first and then my sisters. Mother died. Father shrank; I undertook his care. By the time he died, I was a monolith myself: James and I, triangulated, had a daughter. This familial replication continued, placidly if reviewed in this way: Father, Mother, three children; a difference: two males, three females.

Now an unnatural event. Observed under a microscope, the colony would appear to aberrate. The monoliths move further and further apart until one leaves the field altogether. Now there is one monolith alone, three young; one male, three females. My children grew and, again when we were all about the same size, split off. Then—the replication is so mechanical that I am stupefied—matters continued to develop in this fashion until we, our family, consisted of me (standing there, a weather-beaten monolith), two daughters with husbands, a son, three grandsons; nine of us, six males, three females. Now we are once more reduced. The two husbands have separated. I am still standing in my place, Alexandra in her place with two sons, Mary in her place with one son; Sam moves around the periphery—a lanky, thoughtful man, our sole remaining adult male: three females, four males.

I always liked Julius Caesar's use of the ablative absolute to denote—not describe—action: "The battle won, the soldiers marched." "Their marriages ended, the wives . . ." but I do not know how to end the sentence.

I I   A P R I L

"Their marriages ended, the wives . . ." turned to their children, tended them, and came to recognize that they themselves had produced their most cherished companions.

Enough women used to die in childbirth to render fathers the continuity in their children's lives. Divorce tends to produce the opposite effect: fathers disappear, mothers remain. We are perhaps turning slowly into a matriarchal

49

society. My first reaction to this thought is sadness. I had been trained from childhood to "believe in marriage" and I wore out in it as slowly as I could, with every intention of preserving my family intact, violating virtually every principle of my girlhood except independence of spirit—and that was harried into a corner, beleaguered. The end of my marriage set me free to examine and reexamine my own standards, to reaffirm some, discard some and to form new ones for myself, and for my family. Shortly after my final separation from my husband in 1969, I bought this house in which I live and on the day when it became mine I opened my own front door with my own key, and went straight out to the ground behind the house and lay down on it, among the tall May grasses, knowing it was mine. I rose in strength and though I have looked back, even yearned back, I have never turned back. I realize for the first time as I write that just as earning my own living suits me, so bringing up my own children alone has suited me. Still, a sadness remains. The narcissism of the mother haunts a matriarchal family, rendering it, no matter how broad a context she tries to maintain, a little insipid.

24 APRIL

I first saw my friend who died at dawn this morning on an April evening in 1947, thirty-six years ago almost to the day. A graceful man, witty and tender. A man of sober convictions so deeply held as to need no emphasis other than his life. Now ended, and with it all common recollection of the happy time when this friend of James's was the good shepherd of our early wedded days.

Last week I had dinner in New York with my sister Louise and Alexandra and Mary. We faced one another, crisscross around Alexandra's rectangular table. Louise and I wore flowered dresses and pearls and looked like our mother. Alexandra, black pants and a coarse white cotton lace top; her face was rosy and her hair as classically coiled and as sweetly tendriled as a nineteenth-century marble carving. Mary, a tatterdemalion assemblage: brilliant blues and yellows and greens and whites, flowered and beaded and braceleted as an odalisque.

I am reminded of similar dinners over the years: the listening and the telling. The pleasure of mutual blood, unnameable but unmistakable. The reorganization of our family structure is moving fast. Alexandra, now in the process of legally separating from her husband, will take the first reasonable full-time job she is offered; she has found a steady babysitter, and her two sons are in school. Mary will soon finish a year of graduate work at Hunter College and will start working toward a MFA in writing at Columbia University in the fall; her son, Charlie, is in nursery school. Sam is plowing a straight furrow at Kenyon College. The next generation's heads appeared now and then over the edge of the table: three little boys grinning in the candlelight.

I have been arguing with myself for some months now about whether to take legal action against the University of Maryland on the level of my salary relative to that of other full professors in the Department of Art, all of whom are men. My salary is so significantly lower as to constitute legal inequity, and it has on reflection become clear to me that I would be wrong to submit to it, not only in my own interests but also on behalf of women younger, or in a less secure position, than myself. So I have placed the matter in the hands of my lawyer.

Picasso first touched me when I saw some of his early cubist paintings in a Russian collection exhibited in Tokyo. Standing on tiptoe, I peered over a foreground of smooth, black Japanese heads and saw a strange, new beauty: structure stripped of incident, set free so that I could actually *see* what I had always known existed. A pellucid vision of the forces magnetizing what we name form. A glorious affirmation of the human intellect, as forthright as an intelligent hand placed, on purpose, on my shoulder.

Yesterday Picasso touched me again, but in a different way. The National Gallery of Art is showing the John Hay Whitney collection and there I looked straight into the eyes of a young Picasso—a self-portrait, 1901—and felt his entire presence as if he had stepped into the quiet room where I live with Giotto and Piero della Francesca and Rembrandt, bringing with him a gust of fresh air. As I turned away, changed, my eye encountered *Sleeping Nude,* 1907, the most forthright of all the paintings of women I have ever seen. *No* sentimentality. Such a relief. A man looking at a woman as clearly as he would look at a rock. An eye tender as only detachment can make it. A divine disinterest that allows the woman to breathe her primal breath; her effluvia can be smelt; her power, temporarily stilled, implicit in every stroke on the canvas. *Her* power, not Picasso's. He is in her service, as artists are in the service of truth and nothing else.

Summer

I have just returned from Chicago, where I went for an exhibition of my sculptures and paintings and where I met, for the first time in forty years, an old friend from Bryn Mawr College. When Alice Ryerson walked toward me, arms outstretched, my own opened to meet her with a plenitude of stored affection. We had a wealth of experience to recount to one another during my short visit and we did the best we could with all our facts—our children and grandchildren, our work, our husbands, our conceptions of how our lives had gone and would go. I have felt so diminished lately by the loss of my old friends. No one can take their place, but with Alice I felt a familiar, comforting replenishment.

She lives on the prairie. A swaying, moss-covered log bridge on her land crosses the Skokie River, which drains into the Des Plaines River, which flows into the Illinois River, which in turn joins the Mississippi River. So as I crossed the bridge in the flickering shadows of the forest at high noon, I stepped over the headwaters of the mythical Mississippi, over the bisecting line of the American continent. Trillium sprang from the prairie ground amid a profusion of other wildflowers, among them cattails and the shoots of stout, coarse grasses I was told will become six feet tall. Some part of me is like Antaeus, who drew his strength from the earth, and I have returned doubly fortified, by the American continent as well as by friendship.

14 JUNE

YADDO

SARATOGA SPRINGS,

NEW YORK

Yaddo, an estate to which artists are invited for periods of quiet work, is a measure of change in me because since 1974 I have returned here regularly as a guest and as a member of the corporation.

I have been given the West House tower room again. My bureau is crowded with photographs of my children and grandchildren: the thoughtful faces of young adults juxtaposed with the rosy, eager faces of their offspring. Next to them, the journal a young artist sent me to read, an account of the months preceding the birth of her first child —symbol of the artistic work that now passes through my hands. I process it all with the speed and care of experience, and will mail this journal off today with a note I wrote last night after reading it, so the author will have it back within a week. Foreign cards, too, along the curving shelf under the leaded turret windows: a Piero della Francesca, a Monet that accompanied a photograph of her parents sent me in their memory by the daughter of two dearly beloved friends. My desk is covered with papers I was too tired to cope with last night. A Chinese mug holds pencils and pens and an ivory letter opener that Alexandra gave me; a little Japanese woven basket holds rubber bands and paper clips.

The basket is symbolic. I bought it just before leaving Japan in 1967 for 500 yen, about $1.60. I remember thinking and thinking about buying it. Would I? Wouldn't I? Frittering amazing to me now. And it amazes me, too, that nine years ago, in 1974, when I first walked into this room, I brought nothing pretty or personal—no desk basket, no sewing basket, no photographs, no work of other people, no Japanese cup for flowers, no cards from traveling friends. Books, yes. Always books. But my life was thin then by comparison. Even my reading is different. I read now as an author, with kinship. Mary and Sam are both writing, so we are engaged in habitual literary dialogue.

15 JUNE

". . . there came over her again the feeling she had forgotten, the restful, thoughtless pleasure of a woman who moves in the aura of the man to whom she belongs. As a young woman she had had this unremarkable, yet very precious feeling, when she was with her husband. . . ."* As I used also to have. And in the memory of which I can accept becoming an old woman without it.

*D. H. Lawrence, "The Borderline," in *The Virgin and the Gypsy* (New York: The World Publishing Company, Forum Books Edition, 1944), pp. 265–266.

Two little brown birds with neatly fluted feathers have made a nest between a diamond-paned window in my turret room and its screen. They have fashioned a flattish field of twigs out of which their nest rises on a pleasing scale. The inside is perfectly round, as if a tennis ball had been cut in half, and lined with some loose wood detritus, brownish so that it blends with their feathers. It smells of sunned pine needles. This morning I saw in it one tiny, pale blue egg.

I have started eleven sculptures. Three are square columns varying in height from seven to nine feet, and in width and depth between eight and ten inches. Eight belong in a series I call by the Latin word *Parva* because they are small, not over twenty-one inches tall and ranging from widths of ten to twelve inches and depths of two to five inches.

These are the sculptures that began to appear in my mind's eye last spring. Some artists are able to make their work by a kind of accumulative process—they discover their work as they make it—but I am not. The authenticity of my work depends on an intuitive insight by way of which it presents itself, whole, as if it already existed, somewhere in my mind above my head. In the case of sculptures, I then make scale drawings of their dimensions and have the structures fabricated by a cabinetmaker; they are made of fine-grained $7/8''$ plywood, carefully mitered and splined. They are hollow and if they are tall are weighted at the bottom so that they will not tip. The insides are sprayed with preservative, and they have holes drilled up into their hollows so that they can breathe in various temperatures. I paint these structures with a number of coats, sanding with progressively finer sandpapers between each one, until I have layered color over them in varying proportions. By way of this process, the color is set free into three dimensions, as independent of materiality as I can make it. I have brought bare wood structures here to Yaddo by truck and intend to finish them all while I am here.

I also brought with me thick absorbent Arches paper on which I am making paintings, layers of transparent color superimposed one on another rather as they are in the sculptures.

17 JUNE

A chastening day yesterday. Color rose up and towered over me and advanced toward me. A *tsunami*—only that terrifying Japanese word for tidal wave will do—of color, and I was swept off my feet. In a frenzy, I tried to catch it. Sheet after sheet of Arches paper spread around the studio, covering all the surfaces of all my tables and finally the floor. I tried to keep one step ahead all morning. In the afternoon, I managed to get a toehold, and once again recognized my limitation: that vestige of all that a human being *could* know that is what I *do* know. I see this delicate nerve of myself as unimpressive. The fact is that it is all I have. The richness of years, contained like wine in the goatskin of my body, meets my hand narrowly.

What do I yearn for? I yearn to say what it is to be human but can say only what it is for *me* to be human, a mite. I sit here in my white turret in the gray early morning and force myself to relinquish a dream of expression beyond self. A bitter defeat. Intelligence, which has repeatedly met defeat, falls back to await its hour. But it has to be intelligence informed by a special sensibility that cannot be called up, can only be courted. A state of mind beyond control, a gift of some sort.

The birds are nesting. I now see that the female is plain brown and the male, who comes and goes more, a brighter brown with a soft, Egyptian-red breast. They are tending together this morning, exchanging notes on the day in sounds I cannot decipher. Their single egg makes a pale oval in their round brown nest. Heartened by their sweet sanity, I can think of my studio as a religious might think of a sequestered cell: it is where I do what I can do.

18 JUNE

And so yesterday was a day of alignment, initiated just before I left my room by my discovery of another egg in the nest. Slightly larger than the first, and slightly deeper in color, iridescent, reminiscent of the pale, milky-blue snake in my dreams last summer. Heartened, I set immediately to put color on the sculptures and by the end of the day the three tall columns were becoming visible, and the small *Parva*s were moving in steadily. I am settled for a long pull.

I have noticed over and over that a certain sort of depression presages a jump in my perception of my situation or of my work. Perhaps insight has to be preceded by humility.

22 JUNE

Yesterday I sat down in the studio for about the first time in my life. Reduced to taking the weight off my quaking legs, resting them before mounting my ladders again. I am more bothered by a pain in my hip than I like to admit to myself.

While talking with Alexandra on the telephone, I mentioned the problems I find in this new proportion of relative strengths between me and my sculptures—they are now so much stronger than I, so demanding, and she said, "What are you going to do about them?" I laughed and said, "Solve them, of course!" Of course.

But I am making this new work as if I were never going to make any more.

The question of the equity of my salary at the University of Maryland continues in litigation. My lawyers are moving against the university with due care, so far merely exploring the situation by conferring with university authorities. I so dislike the whole business. But I remain convinced that if a woman situated as I am, in a position of relative strength, does not take a stand against discrimination on the grounds of gender, less fortunate women will be forced to knuckle under to injustice.

If I am turned toward the west when I open my eyes in the morning, my first sight of the world is the trunks of two pine trees tapering straight up from the bottom to the top of a rectangular window. My first act is to move my head a little so as to bring them all into true proportion with one another: two lines in a rectangle. That achieved, I can lie peacefully and for a little while contemplate from the vantage of a rested body a world in what is for me order.

Pantheon Books is printing another edition of *Daybook*.

I am working out ways and means to live with the hurtful right hip that makes it difficult for me to climb up and down my ladders. By changing my lead foot to the left, by moving deliberately, and by gritting my teeth; by putting the heavy sander on the ladder platform before climbing instead of letting it, as I have for twenty years, dangle from my right

59

hand as I mount; by always moving the paint bowl off it before I move the ladder to lighten the weight I have to hoist around a column. All these devices combine to slow me up but, as if in some sweet accommodation, the sculptures themselves are coming in more deliberately, remaining longer in that place from which they approach me. I seem to *hear* them now before they become color, as if sound required color to become visible.

Toth is the name of a tall columnar sculpture I should finish now within three days. Hilda Toth was a medical student twenty-five years old when she was hanged as a revolutionary in the Hungarian uprising of 1956. I saw a photograph of her taken on the day of her sentencing, and felt a strong kinship with her. She looked amazingly like me, the same coloring, and in the tilt of her head as she faced the camera I recognized that of my own when I am trying to be brave.

Another column, *Axilla,* is a narrative sculpture. By "narrative" I mean that its colors vary in hue as they circle the column so that apprehension of the sculpture takes place in time, in a cumulative fashion as the viewer walks around it.

The first veil of color will fall like blue air over the third column, *Australian Solstice,* within the hour; I will brush it on before breakfast.

When I touch my 550-pound Arches paper, I am as absorbed by its rough texture—warm to my fingertips—as the delicate layers of color I paint on its surface. It is as if that surface had depths, like water, into which I were sinking.

My studio is all light and sound now. Four *Parva* sculptures are finished. The three columns loom over me. A table surface is crowded with a miscellany of paint jars; another covered by a drawing board; another for paintings on paper;

another for my typewriter and notebooks. Skylights slant above. Double-winged windows open on a meadow where birds sing among the leaves of apple trees.

The last minute of June last night was counted out at Greenwich, England, the heart of human time, at sixty-one seconds. The insertion of this extra second matches our recorded time with the rotation of the earth, which is slowing down: our day is about two hours longer than a day 150 million years ago. So I suppose 150 million years hence it will be two hours longer than it is now. Even our relation to the sun cannot be, in this long run, counted on as constant.

The other night at dinner we were lightheartedly playing the game of places we would like to be if we could choose freely. What flashed instantly into my mind was the still place I find inside myself when I am most quiet. This is the first time that this inner place has been so appealing; ordinarily my mind's computer spins and comes up with a spot on the face of the earth.

A bird hatched yesterday afternoon. Only as long as the end of my thumb; a few straw-thin bones haphazard around a throbbing heart; a head all beak and blind eyes hanging off a string of wrinkles. Logically, too tiny a complex to live, but the heart beat a drum that the body had to follow and this morning I hear a new voice in my turret.

Had I not seen the bird immediately after hatching, I would be deceived even as soon as today into thinking it had always been a soft, downy creature, all compliability. But I remember the fierce skeleton beneath its fledgling feathers; the character of its nature is etched on my eyeball.

Day after day of steady work is lining with matching failure of endurance the curve drawn on my spirit by the Cumberland Gap drive last December. I get tired very fast. Three hours of work in the morning and I have to drag myself up through the meadow to West House, my lunch, and the nap into which I drop with wholehearted gratitude. I wake up as fresh as one of my grandchildren; catching a glimpse of my face in the bureau mirror, I see it rosy. But by four-thirty I am beginning to check the time—how long I have worked, and how long I have left to work—against my waning energy. A bath and dinner refresh me again. I work after dinner, but an hour and a half later I am relieved to see darkness descend.

There is no place on earth more perfect for working than Yaddo; these conditions are ultimate. Isolated as if in a laboratory, I see that the pattern of my energy has not changed (I have throughout my life enjoyed the naps I used always to have as a child, and gone by choice early to bed) but that its source is drying up. Slowly. But unmistakably.

Up until this year I have flirted with the idea of age, toyed with the role of old woman. During the Cumberland drive, I began to *be* old. The stage lights began to dim. They are out now. The house lights are on. I stand dumb on the dusty proscenium.

Alexandra has been visiting me. She picked out of the paintings I have been making one I had nearly thrown out as ugly; only years of care in the studio and a stubborn trust in my own eye had preserved it from discard. After her departure, I looked at this painting and discerned there a line along which I could advance. A line, furthermore, wide enough for me to develop toward a range of expressiveness I had so painfully relinquished a few weeks ago. It is amazing how work *moves* all on its own. Once again it has taken the lead.

I write at home in my own studio, double doors open onto the alley to catch a vagrant air. The heat is stifling without the relief of the vivid colors that in the tropics match intense heat and fend it off. My garden, except for a few lilies and marigolds, is entirely green, supine under the smothering sun. The tall sculptures I finished at Yaddo stand around me; the *Parva*s and the paintings, still packed, lie on the floor at my feet next to a motley little city of glass jars full of paint.

I sum up Yaddo. In addition to the work I finished, I found a new kind of brush. This is not a minor detail, as my two best finishing brushes, fine-tuned to my hand over ten or so years, are loosening in their handles. And a new kind of relaxation in working, a slower pace because age is making me slower. Art is a presence I am not likely to understand more than I do now; I can rely on that presence if I am unrelenting, patient, and attentive. I see more clearly how my limitation can become my strength if I can give up, once and for all, beating my wings against the cage I have myself, out of my nature and my character, devised to hold my life.

Paradoxically, as I grow quieter in my mind, I am yearning to move around the world. My daydreams have to do with ships and airplanes, with Italy, which I would like to visit next spring when I am due a sabbatical from the university. I am preoccupied by a new curiosity to see for myself lands and seas and art I have hitherto been content to live with in my imagination. It is as if acceptance of my limitation has carried with it its opposite: a desire to see how it might change if exposed to wider experience. I *want* to do that but may be prevented by the economy of my life. I have poured my resources, psychological and financial, into my family and my work; tap as they will, my feet are tied.

Perhaps I should mind that more than I do. I hear Mary and Charlie moving around in the kitchen, across the yard from where I write, and their voices call up in my imagination those of Alexandra and her sons, now in New Hampshire on vacation, and of Sam, who leaves the Bennington College Poetry Workshop this morning for Montreal and Maine. I fly over the territory of my family on wide circling wings, and return to my studio.

8 AUGUST

BETHANY BEACH,
DELAWARE

I hear the ocean's sound: a fall of heavy water and an interval that silence holds intact. I have been coming to this stretch of shore since I was six years old. The waves—mound, curl, break, spume, foam—have been what I have remembered. This time I hear the silence the waves interrupt.

How families can suit one another! Sam wakes up and spreads out his papers on the circular dining table of this brown-shingled rented cottage with a hideous pea-green chimney. Mary emerges from her room and stands in the door with her coffee mug. We pass Sam's writing from hand to hand and comment. Our books are piled on the shelves we have cleared of the owner's belongings: objects of colored glass and driftwood and sea grasses glued together into monstrous marine chimeras. Sam and I are both reading Edgar Lee Masters' *Spoon River Anthology;* it echoes for us the trip to Easton last March when, bearing jonquils, we visited the graveyard in which the generation of my parents lies, more quietly in fact than in my memory. Mary has lent me Gerald Durrell's *Greek Islands,* so I move back and forth from tombs under landlocked Illinois to the Ionian and Aegean seas.

9 AUGUST

The line with which sand grasses articulate their lives speaks of elegance. From a base precisely thick enough to sustain a rise toward the sun without help from the feckless sand, they grow up along a tapering curve until their own force completes a term and they dip gracefully back toward the earth. Their economy reminds me of my mother.

What lessons did her restrained and constricted life teach my delicate and intelligent mother? Perhaps that for all her elegance the pattern of her life was a common one. Her husband drank too much and was not a mate proper to her intellectual station; on the other hand, he tried to be good and this, combined with his unswerving loyalty to her, commanded her affection. Her children were in no way outstanding, though my twin sisters were a distinction, a comfort to ambitions she cloaked with Christian resignation. They were beautiful. Both red-haired, one pre-Raphaelite burnished auburn, the other spun gold, brown and blue eyes to match—a fascinating pair. Cut off from the excitements of worldly success by her modest conventionality as well as by her husband's ineptitude, my mother had to learn to accept the fact that, despite her birth into a family of some wealth and distinction with a broad, entitled view of life, she had fallen into the common denominator of humanity.

My father remained engaged with life to the end—his last words to me were, in a surprisingly brisk voice, "What time is it?"—remained pink in the face, and there was nothing he so much relished as a jaunt. It never, I think, occurred naturally to him that the kernel of a human being is divine. My mother felt this responsibility keenly but she became discouraged in the course of her life and resigned herself to it ever more narrowly, until her death, into which she turned with the confidence that marks brave faith. I have the impression that my father was surprised by the complexity of life, as if it demanded more of him than he had guessed he would need.

On balance—I do not mean to be impertinent to my parents—perhaps Mother came to feel humble despite her natural intelligence, and Father came to feel the importance of a developed intellect despite his natural humility.

They have both been much in my mind during these days at the shore that we visited so often when I was a child. I keep half-expecting them to appear over the dune horizon and join us in what little Charlie calls "the big sandbox."

He is here now, asleep on the other side of the thin wooden partition behind my head. Yesterday Mary and I went by ferry to Cape May to pick him up from his father and grandfather. As we sat over the dinner table, we counted up all the family households in which Charlie is at home, and came to six: his mother's apartment, where he lives; his father's, and his New York grandparents' apartment and beach house; my house in Washington and this house in which we are vacationing. Sammy and Alastair also live with their mother, and are at home with their father and with his parents on Long Island. I am not sure how my grandsons feel about all these monolithic grown-ups with whom they were born connected. The classical emotional environment of Father, Mother, and three children in which I grew up is replaced in their case by what seems to me a baroque plethora of perplexing loyalties.

Alexandra and Mary have not only to balance these conflicts for themselves but also to interpret them rationally for their children in as wholesome a way as possible. They try to avoid deceiving themselves about the natural hostilities with which their marriages ended, and at the same time to suppress them enough to make it easy for their children to be loving within the disparate demands of these extended families. Their situation is further complicated by the fact that they both had their children before they were old enough to have established themselves in the world on their own footing. So they have to combine bringing up their children essentially alone while they work out ways to support them. In addition, they have to take care to provide themselves with working lives that will be enough in character to content them.

13 AUGUST

I was in the kitchen the other day when Sam read me a line of Borges: "You can only lose what you have never had," and I have been thinking it over ever since. The truth is instantly recognizable; it might almost be a platitude. But it came at me at an angle around a corner from his lair of books in Sam's reflective voice, and touched a sore spot in my memory of his father.

For when I mourn, I do mourn what he and I never had: the lovely entire confidence that comes only from innumerable mutual confidences entrusted and examined. And woven by four hands, now trembling, now intent, over and under into a pattern that can surprise both husband and wife. I miss the rich doubling of experience that comes only from such confidence, the nuances of refraction and reflection, nourished and enhanced and underwritten by the sweet union of familiar bodies—touch and smell, tidal.

I mourn my failures to confide. I should have had more courage, dared, risked rejection, even ejection—naked, awkward, crouched as Eve in Masaccio's *Expulsion from Paradise*. "Should" is a dreadful auxiliary word, and worst when linked with "have," rendering an act one never thought of at a certain time, or thought of and decided not to do, as effective and inexorably irrevocable as a deed done.

I mourn what I did not know when I was married: the necessity for honesty between people if mutuality is to bud out of a status quo into air it can then fill with a new form. When I saw how one of the Australian gum trees, the angophora, thrust out new branches, I saw how a marriage could work: a nub pushes out from a fork and as it grows into a branch (these are wide-branched trees) the bark of the tree's trunk spreads smoothly over this rough, crude juncture so that it joins the other branches seamlessly, enhances the whole tree's amplitude. The bark is purple, tan-pink-violet. There is warmth in its seal.

I am saddened that I learned this truth so late, but the ironic fact is that I only came to realize it because of what my children taught me while I was bringing them up alone. The staunchness of their affection and the openness of their hearts slowly brought me to an emotional courage for which I had simply never before had the security.

I mourn because I am now living alone in the light of these insights. The clasped hands of old couples make me sad.

18 AUGUST

When I had the opportunity to buy the house I grew up in, I took it immediately. It all happened easily. My oldest friend, who has never lost touch with Easton, telephoned me to chat one morning and in the course of conversation mentioned that a real estate agent had told her that our house on South Street was for sale. This news instantly locked into the fact that I had just sold five sculptures in rapid succession, and had for the first time in my life a lot of ready money. "I'll buy it," I said casually. "What's her number?" When I reached the agent, she said, "Come on down," so I went on down. I offered $12,500 below the asking price, in cold cash. The owner accepted it. The house was mine. I never even looked at it before I walked toward it as its owner.

The bricks were peeling and needed painting. Pale yellow, as it used to be—I could hear my mother's voice gently demurring with the painter; it was too yellow; paler, please. The ampelopsis she had planted against the vast awkward stretch of the east wall had been ripped out; I would get plants from a familiar greenhouse. Its owner always acted with my father in the Easton Players and would be glad to advise how to space them so that they would cover fast.

My dream faltered here, invaded by my waking mind which began to try to remember this woman's name—Mamie Evans—and as I did I remembered that she was dead and I woke up. But the atmosphere of the dream was so overpowering that I followed it in daydream.

I will repaint the front door and shutters. Dark green to match the lattice my mother had had built around the kitchen yard, and I will buy another Molly Perkins rose to climb there; my mother used to hover anxiously over the one she had planted; it never properly bloomed until after her death, but I will see to it that mine prospers. The garden is deplorable. One or two good gardeners, I decide. Lilacs, as they used to, will flourish in a thriving hedge on the west and I will plant a lavish perennial border all around the expanse of lawn: foxgloves and larkspur, sweet-smelling phlox, and bright blue delphinium. Clumps of hollyhocks and of sunflowers. To the south, along the side of the old carriage house, a spring garden of tulips, scarlet and pink and yellow, and lots of different kinds of jonquils to dance over scilla and grape hyacinth and periwinkle.

I wind around the house on the old brickwork path while I plan, out to South Street and up the steps to the double panels of the front door which I unlock with my own key, reminding myself that I must have duplicates made for my children.

The apartments into which the house has been divided for fifty years must dissolve back into a house undivided against itself. The front hall needs an Oriental runner, crimsons and blues with lacings of green to counterpoint the shadows of the ampelopsis when it spreads up over the two tall slender windows on the east wall. I will move the Victorian mahogany settle now in my Washington living room back here between these windows, and put my grandchildren's little boots into one side where my sisters' and mine

70

used to be kept, and wood into the other, handy as it always was for the living room fireplace.

An awkward living room, saved by the proportion endowed by an eleven-foot ceiling, running along the west wall of the house from two floor-length northern windows in front back to a little catty-corner hall with another fireplace where I used to do my homework at an elegant little French desk. I will paint these walls a very pale blue: a cool restful transition south to the dining room.

I will find another crystal chandelier to hang above the dining table, like the one my parents sold when they sold this house—along with all the Canton china my great-uncle had bought in Hong Kong and the noble decanters in which my grandfather had kept his sherry and port. And Chinese tapestries to replace the ones I remember tracing with my fingertips: raised silken flowers, vines, branches above the formal scalloped waves of a Mandarin sea. I cannot match these but I live a simpler life than my parents. Under my crystal chandelier I will dine on a baked potato, cottage cheese, and a sliced tomato, but I will ask whomever I have caring for me (as our nurses used to, with milk toast, apples, oatmeal cookies, stories, and rough hands) to make homemade ice cream. Strawberry in the spring; peach in the summer, lemon ice; chocolate and vanilla in the winter.

When I walk through these rooms, back toward the kitchen, I see how I can change them even though they are everywhere travestied: the living room and little library hall have long been a shop; the dining room, butler's pantry, and kitchen, an apartment. Space has been scrunched. It all looks mean. Windows dirty, floors scuffed to splinters, here an abandoned bit of rag, there a skim of mould. I summon up the tinkle of the chandelier and the voices of my children and grandchildren and of my guests and their children, and focus back through the crusted pentimento of years to hear my mother and father. They are talking at dinner. There are candles on the table, flickering in the same candlesticks I have on my dining room table in Washington. My mother faces west, my father east. He can see the garden out the southern window, the rows of iris. He won a prize one year for his iris, a silken-bearded monstrous bronze concoction. It was the only honor I can remember his ever having won. My mother is preoccupied. Her voice fades in and out. My father makes a hearty noise. He is starting conversational hares, but my mother will not chase them. Lapses of silence. My mother looks as if she weren't there. My father looks either at the garden or at his pink Minton china plate flanked by heavy, shining silver. When my mother rings the bell for the table to be cleared, I stop watching and listening. That was their marriage I have seen and heard.

As I walk upstairs, my hand on the familiar walnut balustrade, I decide to take the old guest room and bath for my own. I will keep my mother's and father's bedrooms and connecting bath (now with a kitchen, as that space has become an apartment) for my children when they visit. I am glad. They will like that: separation and one roof. Another apartment for them on the third floor, where my sisters and I and our nurse used to live. I do not need to go into any of these rooms. So I say to myself as I mount more and more slowly. I cannot really bear to. I hear low sobbing in my mother's room, and its sound carries through the bathroom into my father's bedroom to resound in the terrible silence with which he somehow contrived to survive his recurrent alcoholic depressions.

So at the top of the steps, I turn due south, into the guest room. Light on three sides. A fireplace on the south wall. I begin to contemplate moving lock, stock, and barrel from Washington. I can make a studio out of the old carriage house in the southwest corner of my garden; there's an alley there and that will work nicely. Then I can spread my furniture over my house, thinly, but I like bare rooms. Anyway —I put off decision—this room *is* my room. White curtains with tiny embroidered flowers like those in my perennial border. A little greenhouse off the south window with a tilted glass roof to catch the sun, and make the rain sound. I will be able to lie in bed at night and listen, and turn snugly into my covers, knowing that in the morning I can light a fire and watch it and read all day if I want to. I will be old here, where I was young.

2 4   A U G U S T

W A S H I N G T O N ,   D . C .

Yesterday I drove to the University of Maryland to try to clear up a graduate student's problem. The fact of my having moved legally to make my salary equitable to that of male professors teaching studio art has changed the air I breathe there. I had not realized how much innocent pleasure I took in feeling approved until I felt the chill of disapproval and a discreet echo of malice. I drove home sick at heart. But last night as I watched my hand running the dishrag over the sink after washing the dinner dishes, a smile took me by surprise. I suddenly understood that I have been more attached to my work at the university, to myself as Professor of Art, than I had known; my pleasure has not been as innocent as I thought. Now, as a result of a probably doomed but nonetheless honest and painstaking effort to right what I feel to be a wrong, I have pierced a bubble of self-deception. As I turned off the light in the kitchen, I felt lighter in spirit and went right to bed and to sleep.

Autumn

My legal resistance to the gender inequity of my salary at the University of Maryland has come to an end. A conference between the opposing lawyers resulted in enough logical clarification of academic governance, of the discrepancy in financial resources between the university (which uses the state's legal services) and me, and of the emotional toll of a prolonged lawsuit, for me to make with reasonable grace the decision to accept the situation. The degree of my relief is a measure of how unnatural bold confrontation is to me. Not even very bold. In effect, I raised my banner, marched up a hummock, listened to reason, lowered my banner, and marched down. Nonetheless, I stood there for the principle of gender equality, and satisfied in myself my personal principle of standing for what I see as right. Wellington, in line with his dictum that a great general knows when to retreat and has the courage to do so, would agree with my decision. Lesser generals, like Custer, die where they stand.

When my children were young and at cross-purposes, I used to take a hand in mine and say, "Hold out your hand facing down," which caught their attention, and then solemnly turn the little hand palm up, with the words, "We'll turn a new leaf."

I feel these days as if I had been turned palm up. My sleep is deep, my days leisurely even when I move swiftly along the halls of the university tending the needs of my students, many more than usual. When things go wrong I don't go along with them, I just step back and wait without making heavy weather of it until I can step forward easily. I am present but, like an incidental figure in a painting, I watch the action in the foreground from a distance.

I note once again that the hallmark of a decision in line with one's character is ease and contentment, and an ample, even provision of natural energy. I am neither a reformer nor a revolutionary. Nor am I an entrepreneur—and this fact I have for the first time clearly recognized, a serendipitous result of my legal confrontation. It is as if that discrete course of events brought into focus a layer of character I have hitherto only subtly known to be treacherous: a real inability to "stand up for my rights." I now perceive that layer in me to be like the Japanese rice papers I used to dye in Tokyo: their texture was so extremely delicate that they rapidly thinned to the point of shred. I can stand up for what I see as "the right," but cannot persist in demanding "my

75

rights." So it follows naturally that I have consistently stood up straight by my work in full view but have only rarely, unevenly, and ineffectively tried to lay claim to the worldly advantages it might, with more deft and able handling, have brought me. I am come to a mind at ease, as if by acceptance of my own nature I have come into tune with some intrinsic ordinance. Acceptance that bears no relation to resignation, the bitter lees of a failure to rise to challenge. For I have found that wholehearted acceptance evokes in me an energy that rises spontaneously when I have carefully examined and come to understand the reality of my character, and have been able to align it with the world around me. As I did last summer when I accepted limitation in my work, and then to my surprise found in that limitation a new freedom.

16 SEPTEMBER

YADDO
SARATOGA SPRINGS,
NEW YORK

Autumn sun burnished the town of Saratoga when I walked around there late yesterday afternoon, endowing it with a look of timelessness that evoked Easton as it exists now in my life, transfixed by the dream and daydream of last month in the amber of memory. Patterned brick and cement squares that sometimes petered out into a weedy verge paved a way for my blue-sneakered feet. Each house along these quiet streets is as individual as a human body of a certain age, someone's decisions writ in its fabric. Distanced at the eyepiece of my experience, I gazed around and wondered about my parents, who had contrived to live in a psychological retreat of their own, distinct like Yaddo, within just such a community. Perhaps the particular ease I feel within the girded grounds of Yaddo is one note in the chord of their legacy to me. For they chose, when they married in 1920, to retreat from the world to the little town of Easton. They made there a life for themselves separated not only from the geography of the world at large in the stubborn provinciality of the Eastern Shore but also from the town itself. Their money, inherited, was an enclave within which they dwelt by choice. I have for years puzzled about this decision. Why did they so remove themselves from the strife and prizes of a larger, more varied, and more interesting world?

By the time of their marriage, Father, forty-one, had lived half his life and in that half had made no professional provision for the rest of his days. The youngest and the cherished baby of six children, he graduated from school in St. Louis and set out, purposelessly as far as I have ever been able to tell, for the Far West. A lively, sociable fellow without intellectual interests, protected by money, he meandered about—cowpoked, worked here and there at whim. When the United States entered the First World War, he went to France as a stretcher-bearer in the Rainbow Division, and when the war ended he married the lady from Boston whom he had met in a grand hotel in Cuba around 1916. An affectionate nature prepared him to be a family man, but his lack of ambition deprived him of a life determined and rounded by the worldly conventions he paradoxically respected. So at the time of his marriage he was in a practical sense crippled by his frivolity, as well as by a more serious disablement: a tendency to depression that periodically drove him to drink. I always remember him being at leisure, so there was never in our household the sustenance of the pattern imposed by a working schedule. When he worked, he did so as a volunteer, cheerfully and generously, but without the daily accumulation of experience that over years in a career lends weight and range to a life. His apparently casual renunciation of these advantages deprived his children of the valuable example of a person making life count.

Mother had lived almost two thirds of her life when she married, at the age of thirty-one. Hers was a life in sharp contrast to my father's. Brought up in the unrelenting discipline of a Boston family separated by only a few generations from Puritan forebears, she had toed the line since her first breath. She declared her independence twice: when she went to Radcliffe College and when she took ship for France as a Red Cross nurse in the First World War. In both decisions she was encouraged by her mother, a strong-minded woman who had been a member of the first class graduated from Smith College. Among my grandmother's principles the service owed by the privileged to the less privileged ranked high. Perhaps Mother's third declaration was her marriage to Father.

During their short engagement, they must have discussed their future and decided to settle near Father's sister, whose husband had taken her home to one of the eighteenth-century river houses on the Eastern Shore. I can now in my own maturity see how this made sense. Practically, because Father would thus simply remove himself from the worldly competition for which he had neither inclination, constitution, nor training; romantically, because at that time the Eastern Shore was so remote as to be exotic; emotionally, because they would move into a place prepared for them by family connections.

And so they married in May 1920 and settled. I was born

in March 1921; my twin sisters in October 1922. We children must have borne for them the weight of all their discarded, disappointed hopes. Certainly we bore a weight. I cannot remember ever as a child having drawn a breath, except when I was alone, that did not deposit in my lungs a sad knowledge. In any case, it is greatly to Mother's and Father's credit that they gallantly and all their lives succeeded in maintaining a household for us that had an atmosphere of high principles and dignity.

The light of these reflections illuminates the disjunctive aspect of my own life that my recent legal foray made clear to me. For all my exertion to achieve, I have chosen almost consistently when confronted by opportunities to win, in the worldly meaning of the word, to be idiosyncratic, to go my own way, to eschew advantage. It is as if I have habitually walked off the playing field of competition, as my father did before me. It is only when distanced from that field— as I am, for example, in my studio—that I pursue a high ambition. I have excellent excuses: I prefer privacy, I scorn showing off, I work best without the world's interruptions. These facts are, however, as true of other artists who succeed in joining high ambition to worldly acumen. I have occasionally wondered if I were lazy, but since this is in all honesty the only area of my life in which I have been so reluctant to act, the reason must lie deeper. Perhaps I drew in with my mother's milk, in that household without a head, an ingrained conviction that recognition was not for the likes of me. Furthermore, that engagement with the world on its own terms was monstrously threatening, because when I was young I never saw it in operation.

The relief following my decision to call a halt to my legal efforts to rectify my university position has been inordinate. I have been surprised by the feeling that in doing so I have behaved in a way profoundly characteristic. I made a statement that stands as made; I withdrew from the pursuit of the possibly very advantageous consequences of that statement. Just as I have made my work in art, and have withdrawn from the pursuit of the advantages with which it might have endowed me in the world.

As I sit here looking out into the apple trees of Yaddo, I ask myself whether this characteristic behavior will change. I doubt it. If worldly success, personified as in medieval legend, approached me gently, laid its head in my lap like a unicorn, I would place my hand on that head and accept its presence. But I do not think I can ever *pursue* it.

15 OCTOBER

WASHINGTON, D.C.

I have not written in this notebook for a long while because I have been silently assimilating. Just as my first grandchild's birth refocused me, the legal turnabout with the university has changed the general attitude with which I live. I feel at once freshly realistic—and to be realistic, to examine facts before feelings, to examine them with sixty-two years of experience, is a fascinating occupation—and freshly appreciative. "Fresh" is the first word describing this new state of mind. "Content" is the next. My students feel it, I think. I have many more students than I have ever had, more eager and more enthusiastic. Art, for a while now stale to my eye, is beginning once again to excite me. I have succumbed to Delacroix: homages to color—passion as tightly coiled throughout his paintings as it is in the prison of our bodies.

In the gesture of turning away from my desk late yesterday after a session of business and university writing, my eye swept across the window overlooking my garden—late tomatoes and white chrysanthemums invisible in the night —and I suddenly realized that I am not going to be able to go to Europe this spring. I had not been thinking about this vague possibility while I worked, but all of a sudden the blocks of my life locked into place one up against the other and their tight alignment spelled a message: I cannot afford to go.

My imagined Italian landscape, painted in my mind's eye when I first laid eyes on Renaissance art, replaced the tomatoes and chrysanthemums, and, as I walked toward the kitchen to heat some soup for supper, I found myself smiling wryly. Tenderly too, for, as far as I can foretell, that lovely little blue and gold and violet landscape of my very own is all I will ever know of Italy.

So much for foretelling. Ramon Osuna, my Washington dealer since 1971, a Cuban of generous heritage, telephoned today and in the course of business about a painting asked me if I had a free week sometime soon; he wants to give me a round-trip ticket to Europe. The idea apparently came to him in the Jeu de Paumes. I *should,* he thinks, see those paintings. I guess he had concluded too that I never would without some drastic action.

Rendered speechless is a phrase too lightly used. All I could do was stammer. "Think about it," Ramon said briskly, adding, with a smile in his voice, "Start to read!"

It would be churlish to refuse. I plan to buy a map-guidebook of Paris in Charlottesville this morning and study it while I have lunch before meeting the members of the faculty who will be in charge of my visit to the University of Virginia. I lecture there tonight. If the bookstore has a copy of Delacroix's *Journals,* I will buy that too, for he could be my brother. But closer than blood: unanimity of spirit. In his footsteps, I have struggled to pull color even further forth out of the context of art, as if all the color in art were a single complexly woven shawl I were drawing out of a pile of clothes. Not for the sake of color itself, but for the sake of what it is to be human, of the emotion, profound beyond explicit expression, from which color implicitly emanates.

In the middle of last night I came up from deeper down in some sea than I have ever been before. As I became conscious, I knew that I had been working steadily for a very long while, intent, concentrated, and that I had been doing this work even deeper down below the cavern of water into which I awoke. I knew that it was time for me to rise through the ice-green dome over my head and seek the shore. I heard the mighty surge all around me, and, knowing that I would need air to go up through the wave, I paused and deliberately took one-two-three deep breaths, then raised my arms and rose up through the dense water. As I broke through spray, I saw where I expected to see it a line of pale yellow sand marking a far strand toward which I began to move. Without bothering to remain conscious, I fell back into sleep.

Twice while I was speaking at the university last night, I felt tears rise to my eyes and almost to my voice. So different from the first time I talked in public at the University of South Carolina in 1974; that echoes in my ear as honest prattle. When I speak now my experience in art wells up so articulately that I am surprised even while I am talking. I move around a podium as easily as if it were my living room and although I am keyed up I am not anxious. I feel as if I were doing what I should be doing—the feeling I have when intent in my studio.

After the talk, I listened carefully while people spoke to me. I notice that though they approach me with a question, they are really asking me to *hear*. I feel this an honor.

This morning I feel the equitable fatigue I now peaceably accept as the inevitable residue of unusual effort. A stabilization toward old age is beginning to be familiar. Just as my evolution from twelve to fourteen taught me what I was going to be able to do, my involution from fifty-nine to sixty-one, akin to adolescence in its erratic energies, has taught me what I am not going to be able to do. The process was the same: knowledge that started as strange and a little frightening ended as natural. Today I will write my bread-and-butter letters, catch up on my business, clean my house,

shop for food, and, in the course of these routine occupa-
tions, work a little on my current sculptures in the studio.

25   OCTOBER

I have been restoring *Seed,* a 1969 sculpture. A column
85" tall by 18" by 18", it is divided vertically into pale rose
and pale yellow. Although the force implicit in proportion
holds these blocks of color together in inflected union, as I
had intended when I first made it, I have realized while
working on it how much more confident my use of color has
become over the years. An ever-increasing emotional freedom, the development of which has not been entirely conscious, has led me to work in color ever more complex and
more delicate in equipoise.

This growth in my work parallels a hard-won, slowly
increasing discrimination and discernment in my life, unfolding, like my fate, as formally as the frond of a fern.

3   NOVEMBER

BRYN   MAWR   COLLEGE
BRYN   MAWR,
PENNSYLVANIA

I have returned here, at the invitation of Bryn Mawr College as Visiting Alumna, to give a talk on my work. The last
time I was here was forty years ago, when I graduated.

It is a brilliant autumn day. I walk around the campus
accompanied by the ghost of myself as I was when I was a
student here, but it is I who feel ghostlike in contrast to this
young self who has risen out of my memory intact, as sturdy

as a peat-bog pony, glossy of pelt and sure of hoof. Her sentences are declarative. Her hopes are her expectations. She walks beside me politely, as if in tacit, slightly deferential acknowledgment that it is I who have met her demands with effort.

The lecture room in which I first saw the paintings of Giotto and Piero della Francesca is obliterated, displaced by an office from which a pleasant, preoccupied woman emerges and brushes past me. The apple tree north of Rhodes Hall, where I lived during my four years of college, is gnarled now; when I was a student, it had but recently come to maturity and in spring its opulent blossoms used to dip over a riotous circle of jonquils blowing in the wind. I climbed the steps of Taylor Hall and sat in my once-assigned seats in classrooms as spare and plain—large windows, wooden desks, scarred podiums, maps, blackboards—as scholarship itself.

Blazing yellow maple leaves against an enamel-blue sky, heraldic colors as compelling as a bugle call, and these utterly blunt classrooms: glory and work. No wonder that at the age of seventeen I fell in love with Bryn Mawr. Like all love, it touched me by way of enchantment, a spell that has lasted in the form of gratitude for the spine of discipline along which I have worked ever since.

5 NOVEMBER

WASHINGTON, D.C.

Mary and Charlie flew down unexpectedly yesterday and now I wait for them to wake up so Mary and I can talk some more and Chooch and I can read some more: we cuddle close and warm and chat over *Frog and Toad.* Frog and Toad are more sophisticated than Little Bear, who is very much a homebody, a traditional child safe with Mother Bear and Father Bear. Neither Frog nor Toad have families. They are quasi-adults. Each has a house, and quirks. Their friendship has ups and downs as real as their mutual affection. Without any hint of sexuality, they act out *relationship,* the central emotional problem that Arnold Lobel's readers face in their adjustment to the lives of the adults around them. Frog and Toad say "We disagree" and "We are friends" without either statement contradicting the other. They say that affection abides conflict.

10 NOVEMBER

A percipient friend who treats my hip and gives me nutritional advice (I am having difficulty taking food seriously) remarked yesterday that I might be thinking of myself as worth more dead than alive. In money, I am. No doubt about that. My life translated into cash would place a tidy sum into the hands of each of my children. Alive, I am likely to cost them. I do not have enough to live on without my teaching salary and that's scary, as I do not know how long I will have the strength to teach. I could sell my establishment and sustain breath in my body (I think) on the income from the principal thus realized. Bearing my lares and penates with me, I could make myself another home. But to lose my studio would be a little death.

Not yet. My intention is to be a vigorous old woman. So I must learn how to take the different kind of care needed by the worn envelope in which I now live, and must summon up the motivation to do so. What complicates the matter is that along with the physical changes of approaching old age a psychological balance in me has tipped: I recently have perceived that the tiny flame I most reductively and truly am is not going to flicker out. I *am,* and that's that. Instead of my experiencing *my* flickering out in death and *life* going on without me, as if dying would dragoon me from a drama in which I was playing an interesting part, I will simply slip out and take my self with me. So staying alive in this chafing physical envelope—stiff as cardboard here and thin as tissue paper there—is no longer entirely essential to the continuity of my existence. In fact, I begin to see being alive as being caught in a fix. My body is no more and no less substantive than the ever-moving panorama my sensory apparatus formulates for me and beguiles me with: *tick-tick-tick*—each second caught out of nonexistence into existence, lost again to nonexistence as soon as perceived. A mechanical process. I name it my life. And around me other people organize their own printouts to call their lives. Similarly constituted, our sensoria are sufficiently in common to prevent total chaos; but each individual system is enough out of synchronization with every other to guarantee a degree of disorder.

When I was younger, I saw the variety as infinitely interesting. I still am fascinated by how it all dovetails, so narrowly. We lumber and stumble and bump and grope, but, carefully examined, each of our lives makes sense. We develop in ways we can discern as teleological if we do not throw up our hands in consternation, impatience, or despair. I think one of the reasons we have difficulty seeing this teleology in the perplexities of our lives as we live them is because we do not know a context in which it could be recognized as logical. The facts of examined experience, however, postulate such a context.

In my freshman year of college, I went to Baltimore to visit
for the Thanksgiving vacation. My appendix burst and I
spent six weeks at Johns Hopkins Hospital. In those days
there were no antibiotics and after the operation I lay on my
back with wide-bore macaroni-like tubes protruding from
an open incision. The peritoneal infection was supposed to
drain out these tubes, and began to do so in reasonable
enough order for my mother, who unremittingly worried
about money, to have me moved to a double room from my
single room where, by turning my head (the only motion
I could make without hurting), I could see from my high
bed a triangle of sky above the building opposite my hospital wing, and a polygon of green grass. My new room was
on the other side of the wing. A brick wall a few feet from
the window clamped off all space. I saw this instantly as the
nurses wheeled my bed, accompanied by a white iron pole
from which a bottle of saline solution dripped into my hand,
and fitted it in next to the bed of the stranger who lay by
the window.

I grasped the facts: my helplessness; the close dark slot
which was my half of the room; my mother's economy both
of energy (she had only a meager little beyond that required
to adjust to the circumstances of my catastrophe, which had
delivered her alone into an unfamiliar city, cut off from her
secure routine) and of money (a fearful meanness); the
claws of pain from which I had held myself aloof by weaving
the filaments of my character into a sort of safety net. These
facts seized me, grasped me in iron prongs, and hoisted me
beyond the reach of my imagination. I cried. I made a scene.
I hear myself screaming. The nurses rushed around my bed.
My mother stood off beside the door. I see her now, a
slender, thin-boned, dignified lady, her hand to her mouth

in consternation, but beneath the consternation I recognized the inexorable force of her will: she had made a decision. I was going to have to adjust. I remember clutching a nurse to save me, starched white cotton under my hands making wrinkles. The doctor was called. I had twisted the tubes hanging out of my side. Somehow order was restored.

And then in my memory my mother sits by my side, dim-lit, erect, on a straight chair. She is reading and looks relieved. *I* am going away. I have actually gone, borne on a slow, full tide. I do not see a shore. I remember half-thinking, "It isn't worth it. I won't bother to stay." And so, quite without regret, I let go. My temperature shot up (I heard the doctors worrying about it from the citadel of my indifference). Occasionally tears of weakness wet my face but not for long; I soon accepted twilight as serenely as my mother read in her chair by my bed. Quite quietly dying, I would have died had not my great-aunt sent my mother a large sum of money. Mother would not have noticed, I think, until too late. As it was, the money came and I was moved back into my old room. When they had all gone and I was alone and silent with air and light and space around me, I turned my head and looked out the window. I saw the triangle of sky, blue, and an unmarked white polygon of fresh snow over the grass. "If I get well," a small voice announced way inside my head, "I can take a walk in the snow and eat a red apple." And so I did.

This turn from despair into hope is one I have made repeatedly throughout my life. Sometimes by way of money received like that from my great-aunt, or from foundations in the form of grants; sometimes because I have been heartened by a word; sometimes a spring of faith rises from within myself. All equally gifts; warrants of divine protection.

Winter

Alexandra will be twenty-eight years old at 7:13 this evening.

Her two sons and I were at the Museum of Natural History in New York last week examining the African animals when all of a sudden Sammy, who is now five and very much the older brother of Alastair, veered off. Without a word he settled himself on a bench running around under the stuffed trumpeting elephants in the center of the gallery, unbuckled his backpack and, gently putting to one side the floppy anonymous animal he had fixed so that it could look from under the canvas flap to see the sights, deliberately slid some papers out of the pack. I sat down beside him. Alastair leaned against me. We watched silently. Sammy took his time. Digging out a stub of crayon, he drew without hesitation; in a minute, he said, "See," without any emphasis, and Alastair and I saw that he had drawn one of the exhibits—striped horselike animals with horns amid stripes of jungle trees. I said, "Oh, good, Sammy." Alastair pushed appreciatively against our knees. Sammy looked at his drawing a second and then silently reversed all his procedure until his crayon was back in its pocket, the papers flat, and his animal comfortably rebuckled so he could see out. When Sammy stood up, I did too, took Alastair's ready hand and we pushed through a snowy blizzard home to lunch.

Actually, I scarcely glanced at the drawing, of which I had little hope. But it stays in my mind, echoing the surprise with which in that glance I took in stripe of animal and stripe of tree locked in a startlingly tight abstraction. The whole sequence was authentic. Sammy wasn't showing off; I wasn't thinking he was cute; Alastair was his usual little humming dynamo; even the drawing was austere. I feel in some way taken aback, and taken back too: to the first moment I looked at Sammy just after his birth. Wordless. Respectful. I take it for granted that everyone and everything around me is moving entirely independently of any reference to me, so I looked at Sammy's drawing impartially. I failed to recognize immediately that in this instance my grandson was like me: a person who wanted to make his experience real for others and who set about to do so.

11 DECEMBER

Sam and I once agreed that even when we part from the people we most love, there is in the moment when we turn our backs a subtle lift of spirit. He wondered whether death was like that and we decided that it probably is—as if a falcon, untethered, soared.

But it is life, not death, that is untethering me. As the time for my departure for Europe approaches—I plan to leave in January—I am becoming excited. My sabbatical from the university begins in two days: a baker's dozen of months, thirteen. Not a big slice of a life but notable in proportion to the number of vigorous years I have left, at sixty-two, to live. I am also seriously considering a change beyond that of the trip to Europe. Curtis Harnack, the executive director of Yaddo, is anxious to go on a leave of absence for nine months. He would like me to take his place as acting executive director for that period of time—April through December of 1984. I am inclined to do so.

Yaddo is an institution for which I have the utmost respect, as well as affection. In 1881, Spencer and Katrina Trask bought a tract of land over four hundred acres broad, comprising a large house, a number of miscellaneous farm buildings, and four lakes, and retreated there from New York after the death of their oldest child. This shadow lay over them, and a daughter suggested they name the place "Yaddo" because it rhymed with "shadow" but to her mind suggested its opposite, as indeed it turned out to do: in Old English "Yaddo" means "shimmer"—light on water. After the tragic deaths of all their children, Katrina Trask conceived the idea that Yaddo be preserved as a retreat for "literary men, literary women, and other artists . . . who are weary, who are thirsting for the country, who are hemmed in by circumstances and have no opportunity to make for themselves a harmonious environment." She and her husband set up the Corporation of Yaddo, and after their deaths, Yaddo opened its doors in 1926 to artists invited to come there and work.

Selected by a panel of their peers, they are, in accordance with the laws of the corporation, guests. They pay nothing for the privilege of making visits, which now range in length from four to eight weeks. Over the years a schedule has evolved: guests have breakfast together, pick up thermoses and pails of food for lunch, and have a communal dinner at six-thirty. Silence is observed from nine o'clock to four o'clock; personal messages are taken by the office so that the guests are assured of working time free from even the possibility of interruption. I have been a guest there four times since 1974, and fully appreciate the unique ease that these conditions provide for working; for interchange also, as the artists are poets, novelists, composers, photographers, painters, sculptors. Their visits overlap so this cross-fertilization has maximum flexibility. I have never come away from a visit without having accomplished an amount of work that astonished me, as well as having met interesting people, at least one or two of whom have remained permanent friends.

The job of acting executive director would be a challenge: I would be handling a great many administrative details, ranging from the problems that occasionally arise with guests through housekeeping matters and work on the grounds to the financial structure that keeps it all going. I have been a member of the corporation since 1977 and a director since 1980. Curtis Harnack and I are compatible. I have seen how he likes Yaddo to be run, and although I would not do the job the same way he does, I feel that I could walk in my own shoes in his footsteps.

Another factor inclines me to accept. During my thirteenth year both my father and my mother were so sick that the care of our household—parents, sisters, nurse, servants —descended to me. I was young and inexperienced and scared. I had to pretend that I knew what I was doing, which in itself is frightening. My ego inflated when this pretense was accepted—when, for example, the cook took my orders as calmly as I had watched her take my mother's—but it swelled like a blister over the raw knowledge that I really was not adequate to the responsibility. In behaving as well as I could under this pressure, I grew accustomed to pretense: the pattern of rising to challenge by pretending that I could meet it squarely and then trying to hide my anxiety while I learned how to do so. This is not a healthy pattern. The job of acting executive director of Yaddo would give me an opportunity to meet new, wide responsibilities without having to resort to it, because I would be meeting them in my maturity.

A stale feeling underlies logic. I have lived in this house for fourteen years. Particularly since the departure of my children from under my roof, I am becoming set in my ways, and I find that my ways are in turn setting around me like a cement garment.

15 DECEMBER

In the end, my deliberations were tipped by my loyalty to Yaddo, as well as by a decision to cast off stasis. In our meeting this week in New York, the Yaddo board of directors voted Curtis Harnack a leave of absence. I was appointed acting executive director to serve from 1 April to 31 December 1984.

I am full of pleasurable expectations. I will spend the last two weeks of January in Paris, and then go on to Italy to visit an old friend who lives in Asolo, north of Venice. Now that I have accepted the position at Yaddo, I see that even these excitements would not have been enough to give me the change I need. Nine months at Yaddo will do that. I have rented my house for that period and am turning an eye toward its preparation when I return from Europe. I am also beginning to contemplate Yaddo from the angle of responsibility and find the view evocative.

I am reviewing French.

In Beginning French at St.-Genevieve-of-the-Pines in Asheville, North Carolina, a convent school founded by nuns whose Mother House (delightful phrase) was in Belgium, we read *La Tâche du Petit Pierre.* The nun who taught us cried when Pierre confronted the task of climbing down a steep rock cliff to rescue his cousin, fallen and hurt on a strip of beach rapidly narrowing in an incoming tide. Even as my heart went out to her, I wondered why our teacher cried about this banal tale. Her tears were painfully honest; I can see them now coursing down the wrinkles on her pale, slightly yellowish cheeks. I saw in her a strained resignation akin to my mother's and made up my mind then and there to guard myself against it.

We progressed to the instruction of a brisk Bretagne nun with short-fingered, quick little hands and round, very red cheeks like apples pushed against the wings of her wimple. And to Pierre Loti's *Pêcheur d'Islande,* which made *me* cry. Yann, a young fisherman, marries just before departing on a voyage. When, after some months of separation, his vessel is due, his wife begins to wait for him. She watches for a sail from the headland. She lies sleepless, listening for him, and at last, one night when his ship is so long overdue that everyone else has given up hope, she hears his step coming toward her room. She is certain it is he and the weight of her anxiety lifts as if it had never lain heavy on her. She turns in her bed to welcome him home. The steps pass her door. She never hopes again.

In the years since I read this sad story, I have lain many a night waiting for beloved people to return. Last night Sam's plane from college was late. I listened for his key in the door and time went on, but as I lay there quietly an unlooked-for tide of comfort rose slowly to float the barque of my fearful imagination. Worry is a form of blasphemy, a substitution of one's own will for divine will; actually, a clumsy attempt to usurp divine power. But I have often thought that before and been unable to absorb this insight, because when I get worried I tend to think of my children as very young. Last night my common sense asserted itself. Sam is a competent fellow; if vague by nature of his preoccupations, he is reasonably alert to his own preservation. All very well, and I hope that I will be able to remember these facts, but I was nonetheless infinitely relieved when I heard his step on the porch.

I will not be able to remember. I remain irreducibly vulnerable to my children, as, in a lesser degree, to my work.

I just turned out my lamp to look for dawn through the refractions of frosted windows. A faint blue light, and I am glad. I sometimes wonder what it would be like if the sun simply never came up, as Yann simply never came home.

2 5   D E C E M B E R
C H R I S T M A S   D A Y

Behind my head in the room next to mine, rustlings like mouse thumps announce that my grandchildren are opening their stockings. It is five-thirty A.M. The fathers telephoned last night to speak to their children. Sammy and Alastair will be picked up today by their father, who will fly them back to New York for a second celebration with his parents.

This is the Christmas of reality for my children and me. We have all, with varying degrees of reluctance, abandoned the fiber we wove among and around us to keep us while the children grew to maturity. The eleven years since Alexandra was seventeen have so loosened and thinned this nest that most of it has blown away in wisps. We can afford anger now and a certain crossness has made this Christmas convocation a little tart. A healthy feeling.

Sam and I took the three little boys to the children's service at the National Cathedral near our house yesterday afternoon. Stuffed into our puffy down jackets, helmeted and mittened against a bitter wind, we buffeted our way up and back in a happy Dickensian procession of folk young and old. With a watchful eye on our three tots who were seated among others on the cathedral floor at the base of the poinsettia-garlanded pulpit, I watched the shadow of the high crucifix deepen against the vaulted ceiling and the blues in the north rose-window fade against the darkening afternoon.

"Blue is your color, Annie," I used to be told when I was a child, and so it has been in my work.

The Egyptian blue of antiquity was the result of a high-temperature fusion of copper silicates. In the melee of history, this method was lost for a long time and artists were largely reduced to the colors of ordinary earth minerals: ochers, umbers, carmines, viridians. In the eleventh century, travel between West and East increased. Artists heard tell of a blue stone mined somewhere deep in Asia, and in the thirteenth century Marco Polo was so curious about this persistent rumor that he went out of his way to the snowy headlands of the Kokcha River in Afghanistan and found the legendary mines. So chunks of lapis lazuli were soon added to the loads carried by camels along the ancient Silk

Route, and shipped on to Venice. When the stones were crushed and the fool's gold removed, the remaining pure blue was ground into a fine powder called ultramarine (literally "from beyond the sea") which could be mixed with various binding media and used as paint. More costly than gold, a color was for once rated high enough, justly valued for beauty alone.

Today I start restoring *Sentinel* for the Allbright-Knox Museum. I will add that remuneration to the little pile of gold I am accumulating for my travels—a modest bulge in the leather purse with strings I have imagined for it. Two friends have loyally contributed by buying work: a drawing, a sculpture; Ramon Osuna has generously either refused or halved his commissions on these sales.

I am deliberately loosening my feet from the American soil in which I was planted at birth and on which I have always counted for strength and nourishment. It is as if I have drawn up, literally *up* through my feet, from that earth, a kind of force that has made a seed somewhere under my heart. I *carry* that. It belongs to me by right of watchful attention and keeps me company as if it were one of my sculptures, but different in texture, flesh of my flesh, whereas the sculptures are bone of my bone.

Now I do not feel excited as much as matter-of-fact and *right:* I know that I am going to see with my own eyes the history of my own kind. A history that I will absorb as in some mysterious way lapis lazuli attracted unto itself, and retained in itself, blueness. I will myself be ultramarine— "from beyond the sea."

This trip will set at variance my tendency to retrace my

own steps in an attempt to reenforce my personal history by repeated overlays of experience—as if I had dreamed my past and had to affirm it. This impulse has led me to return to Easton, Maryland, over and over; to Virginia; to Asheville, North Carolina; to Boston; to New York. And also to return in dreams. I wonder if the change I am feeling is a turn into the present, and thence into my own future. The remarkably vivid and consecutive dream I had last August about reclaiming the Easton house in which I grew up seems to have closed the gestalt of my childhood. It is as if an imaginative lasso had been flung out by my unconscious to collect my past into my present. I have not dreamed of Easton since, nor of my childhood. On this trip, I am myself moving out on a loop into the history of humankind, an impersonal history, rich with personal unknowns.

The last time I went out on such a long journey was in 1981, when the Australia Arts Council invited me to lecture on my work. Although there were plenty of cogent reasons to accept this invitation, my principal motivation in going was to fly once more back and forth over the Pacific Ocean. I lived in Japan from 1964 to 1967, and during that period flew this ocean six times—the only times in my life when I had *enough* space and *enough* blue. In 1981 I still hoped to match in "real life" the immensity of a context that I was very slowly beginning to intuit just beyond the ordinary range of my consciousness.

The Australian Aboriginal custom of walkabout reflected with uncanny precision my bone-deep obsession with tracking myself. Each Aboriginal is by tradition born into a phylum, a primary category of the animal kingdom. At intervals devout Aboriginals go walkabout: they visit sacred places on the original paths made by their most remote forebears. They draw strength, and knowledge too, from placing their own feet, physically, in their forebears' tracks. This makes perfect sense to me.

The continent of Australia was made magical for me by this idea. And this magic was reenforced in macrocosm by the extraordinary placement of the continent: so isolated by the great sea entirely surrounding it that it takes on a stubborn indomitability. A slab of red-orange rock with a fringe of green, set all alone in measureless, ceaselessly moving blue water, flooded with light from the most golden sun I have ever seen. A wind, unstopped by any other land down there between the 50° and 40° latitudes, sweeps over a broad, flat expanse as dry as dry can be, much of it "Gibber" plain: sand set with gibbers, red-purple rocks ranging from the size of pebbles to that of small boulders. Cruel to the human foot, indifferent to the human eye, the continent resists any imposition of human scale. By way of a sense not sensory, I heard it sound: a chord of high sweet music I picked up through my feet.

In Australia I found a physical reality complexly wrought of elements at their ultimate: space of air and earth and sea; color; sound. I did not find, even in this context of ultimate elements, any equivalent remotely matching the expansion I was tentatively experiencing in my own consciousness. I came to realize that this kind of experience is an end in itself.

1984

Yesterday the two curators of twentieth-century art and the chief conservator of the National Gallery invited me to lunch so that I could tell them how to clean my sculpture, *Spume,* which has become dirty since acquired in 1972. We met at the entrance of the east wing and went straight to the gallery in which they are planning to install *Spume.*

One hundred twenty inches tall by 25½″ wide by 13½″ deep, luminescent blues and violets, it loomed over me. I straightened up to face it. In the first second of looking, I did not recognize it as my own work and only felt its presence, with an involuntary shudder. I was so taken aback that I rocked on my feet. "What on earth—?" were the first words that came into my mind, along with the very particular sharp tension I sometimes feel while I am making my work: as if I were being forced face to face with a mystery equally threatening and alluring.

Pulling myself together, I put my hands in my pockets (they had theirs in theirs) and brought my attention to bear on the questions they were asking me. Practical men with an object to deal with, they wanted information. How had the structure of the sculpture been fabricated? What sort of wood had been used? What kind of paint? How many coats? How applied? How could the smudges on its surface best be cleaned? When I said that I used soap and water, finally wiped down with a clean, damp cloth in the same long continuous strokes with which I applied the paint, they looked disconcerted. They are accustomed to more recondite restoration processes. We proceeded to lunch, during which the gentlemen leaned back in their chairs and spoke of great artists long dead whom they were apotheosizing by exhibiting. Their easy discussion of what they were doing with works of art so bypassed the artist's effort that I walked away from the gallery feeling that that effort had been discounted. Artists die; their work survives to be handled as others see fit. I have always known this fact, but never before had the triumph of the living over the dead been so plainly demonstrated to me.

I had also recognized once again that my sculpture is a bother because it is large and has a delicate surface. Despite years of self-discipline, I can never entirely avoid identification with my work and when it is thought bothersome I feel as if I were myself criticized. I have thought a lot about this aspect of my work and wonder sometimes if the vulnerability of my sculptures does not combine with their size to awaken the subtle hostilities evoked when women retain innate delicacy even while asserting their existence.

I bought my house in 1969, and in 1971, when the plot was surveyed to build the studio in my backyard, I discovered that the fence between my land and my neighbor's to the south was not on the line of our properties. My neighbor, who had sold me the house, had allowed the fence to stand because it gave me, her friend, eighteen more inches of garden. Last month we were simultaneously seized by a desire to make our properties shipshape for our descendants and decided to share the expense of a new, accurately surveyed fence. Now it marches between us in peeled sapling poles evoking the innocence and terror of Colonial American stockades, but for a few hours yesterday the land lay open. Our houses squared off one another in a lovely, natural way, each dignified in the scale suggested by an uninterrupted horizontal. The line of the old fence was discernible in a straggle of vines, but it was easy to see that a month or so would knit the landscape together. The houses had nothing to do with the fence. Aloof on the bare land, each occupied its own due proportion. And under them, rich, smelling of fecund secret winter, rolled the indifferent earth.

I looked up the Church of St.-Julien-le-Pauvre in my new *Michelin Vert* with the innocence of Marcel Proust lifting the cup of lime-flower infusion to his lips. I read: "Small local church in a picturesque setting and an unforgettable view of Notre-Dame."* The view has three stars and I remembered

*Michelin, *Green Guide to Paris* (1981), p. 99.

my mother's melodious voice explaining how Baedeker guides rated with stars, and thought of her familiarity with Paris, with France, where she went almost every summer of her adult life until she married my father. The Michelin guide continued: "Chapels have stood on this self-same site since the sixth century. Several of them have been named after St. Julien, Bishop of Brioude in the third century; others after the Medieval Bishop of Le Mans who gave away everything he had and hence was poor; others after the ferryman and Hospitalier"—the site is immediately across the River Seine from Notre-Dame, on the Isle de la Cité. The present church is named after the medieval bishop: St. Julien the Poor. It was built between 1165 and 1220, at the same time as Notre-Dame, on which construction started in 1163.

"Since the sixth century"—fifty years after Attila the Hun in 451 streaked across the Rhine with his ravening horde, my first childhood image of blazing violence set loose on purpose, of inordinate ambition sanctioned by power. The Bishop of Brioude was martyred in the third century, two hundred years before that. "The ferryman and Hospitalier" (not otherwise identified by Michelin), one of the sorts of people who set practically about daily business—transport and healing. I wanted to imagine how he might have looked, turned to the historical notes and found that I could think of him dressed in skins, poling a coracle. The Parisii, fishermen and boatmen, settled on the Ile de la Cité between 250 B.C. and 200 B.C. They named their collection of huts Lutetia, in Celtic, "habitation surrounded by water." They were *Gauls*—the sound crawls in my backbone. Julius Caesar's Gauls, my own Gauls, belonging to me by right of my imagination, hotly engaged with Julius Caesar's campaigns when I was fourteen. Conquered by Roman Legions (not under Caesar, under Labienus) in 52 B.C., so Lutetia became a Gallo-Roman town, now the Latin Quarter. The boatmen worshiped on the site of Notre-Dame, under which a pagan altar has been discovered: I can *touch* that altar, maybe, with my hand, touch all that *time.* My feet will imprint on the soil of Paris another overlay on millions of layers of human feet back to 250 B.C. As I read I felt with a surge of insight the actual continuity of humankind. A recognition I had not forcefully confronted since my mother and I walked through Westminster Abbey in London when I was ten years old.

I am taken aback. I feel as if I had fallen into a bottomless hole of past, for what I touch I know to be actual, and if this stretch of time behind the Church of St.-Julien-le-Pauvre into which I shall walk is truly real, the time before this stretch is also real, and the time after it, as well as the time after my lifetime. I leap, emotionally, to the side of Marcel Proust and see with more than my mind—which suddenly seems to me to have comprehended no more the reality of time than that symbolized by the thickness of a sheet of paper—why he was obsessed by time and why he prowled the churches of France. Why his Narrator in *A la Recherche du Temps Perdu* gazed when a child at the Duchesse de Guermantes in the church at Combray, and fell in love with her because she sat in the Chapel of Gilbert the Bad where "beneath . . . flat tombstones, yellowed and bulging like cells of honey in a comb, rested the bones of the old Counts of Brabant."* She *embodied* the past, like a heraldic device. "Great and glorious before the days of Charlemagne, the Guermantes had the right of life and death over their vas-

*Marcel Proust, *Remembrance of Things Past* (New York: Modern Library, Random House, 1928), p. 224.

sals; the Duchesse de Guermantes descends from Geneviève de Brabant."*

The name Geneviève runs like a bright green thread through the centuries my mind is stretching to span. It was Geneviève, a young religious, who in 451 assured the inhabitants of Lutetia, by that time for one hundred years named Paris, that Attila would turn aside from its borders, and so he did; when the island was besieged by the Franks in 461, Geneviève made her way secretly to Champagne and returned safely with provisions. When she died in 512, she was buried beside King Clovis—Clovis, another of my childhood touchstones, "good" as opposed to Attila's "bad." The remains of her bones are contained within a shrine in St.-Etienne-du-Mont Church, where I shall go and stand and know they are there: fifteen-hundred-odd years of time embodied in shards of her skeleton, the familiar, often drawn structure that once informed her body as mine does my own.

The school in which I learned the French language and read about the Gauls was named for St. Geneviève. In Asheville, North Carolina: a settlement of houses, as primitive esthetically as those of Lutetia, scattered randomly along the crude, humped flanks of mountains, still virgin forests; a town about one hundred years old in 1937, the year of my graduation, so about equivalent to 100 B.C. in Lutetia's time. The Belgian and French nuns who ran the school were *missionaries*, exiled to our frontier to spread the Catholic faith in the wilderness. When Reverend Mère spoke the words "Saint Geneviève," her thin, pale lips used to linger sensuously over the syllables. I can now grasp a little of what she may have felt these syllables evoked: her

*Proust, *op. cit.*, p. 226.

civilization entwined with her faith, for she herself was as much an embodiment of a culture we heathen children could not even begin to guess as the Duchesse de Guermantes.

As I write, I see my mother's face too, her gray-blue eyes always a little remote, and feel as if I had abruptly entered the realm in which she dwelt, and encountered her reflectively walking there. It was this perspective, time, to which I am coming so late in my life, that lent intelligence and grace to her point of view. Her loneliness smites me. She was as exiled in Asheville as Reverend Mère. She had no friends there. She held herself aloof even from acquaintances. Even from her children. I remember returning late from an evening out when I was on vacation from college; when I went into her room to let her know that I was home, she was lying flat on her bed wide awake, her eyes colorless in the moonlight that lit the room. We exchanged a few words; when I turned away I left her there, as still as an effigy. When I learned a year later that she was dying of a brain tumor, this image of her flashed across my mind: in some way, even beyond the reach of the child of her own body, she had repelled intimacy as if in some fastidious decree of her intelligence she had made up her mind that she would never be able to express what her life meant to her, and had best acquiesce to that fact with the dignity of resignation. It was so that she died, slipping quietly from a mute life into the silence of death. Were we to meet now, in my own maturity, she might come to trust herself to me, and I myself to her. But the sad fact is that she died when I was twenty.

I am reading *King Lear*. On face, a rattling good yarn; one rash action after another, *rat-a-tat-tat*, scarcely halted by Cordelia, Kent, and the Fool. Gloucester, despite his gruesome fate, remains unsympathetic—it is hard to take an interest in anyone so instantaneously, and on such trivial grounds, disloyal to a son—but I recognize Lear instantly. I have often observed how a spasm of middle-aged indiscretion has laid lives to waste.

At this turning point in life an avidity for change may be one form of adjustment to the foreshadow of death. An adjustment that substitutes for acceptance a surge of willfulness. Over and over, I have seen people at this age, apparently hemorrhaging in some inarticulate aspiration, become restless and cast about recklessly for *any* sort of change, as someone in mortal pain thrashes on a sickbed. Unable or unwilling to make psychic changes that take death into account, a person instead makes abrupt changes in circumstances and often loses the good of the knowledge accumulated in the steady effort of a lifetime. Thus diminished, a life can trail away in small busyness. Amusements become the equivalents of Lear's knights: memories, hobbies, anecdotes of erstwhile cronies and skirmishes, creeping self-indulgences. This turn of events can make a person foolish, in need of a Fool to mirror lost self-respect.

I have been experiencing a mild form of this restlessness myself lately. I look to this sabbatical year of change to meet it intelligently.

Last night I was awakened by the wail of a train whistle way off to the east where the steel lines, along which I have traveled north and south all my life, cross and crisscross up and down the East Coast. Its echo trailing off in my ear and memory made me resolve that I am not going to be seduced by the ancient riches of time away from my very own native land. I do not belong to St.-Julien-le-Pauvre, St.-Geneviève, or the ghosts of the Parisii. If I were an echo, I would by birthright linger over the broad stretches of the American continent.

19 JANUARY

I fly away from it on the night of 23 January. Five more preparatory days. I am stripping my house for the friends who will live in it for the month I will be in Europe; soon it will look like the shell it has always been, a dwelling ready for changing habitation. Equally stripped, I will be off with as little as will make me viable. That is a good feeling. I know that as my foot crosses the threshold of the airplane, my spirit will lift, for from that second on I will be alone in the liberating anonymity that travel confers. Now I cling to my domesticity, counting off the rosary of my days under my own roof, crouching in my habits, enjoying little customary pleasures and waiting, almost with a feeling of resignation, for the wind to pick me up.

In my *Michelin Vert,* I have scouted out the topography of Paris so that when I arrive I can align myself north, south, east, west. And I continue to review French. I remember *not* memorizing the days of the week at St.-Genevieve's, and now I have to learn them—an example of how life never lets us off the hook. My notebook fits nicely with Delacroix's *Journal* into one side of a carry-on valise; in the other side, a cashmere sweater and a pink-striped traveling kit. French money is engraved with the portraits of *artists:* Delacroix, De la Tour, Montesquieu, Debussy; I am astounded, and catch a distant trumpet of an entirely new point of view. I wonder if, by way of similar extraordinary facts I cannot predict, I may feel more at home in Europe than on my deeply loved stretches of land here. Something stubborn in me hopes not, and in recognizing that part of me I suddenly know why I never sought out Europe when, for years of my life, I had ample opportunity: I am afraid of its wisdoms, leery of challenge to the little developments of my own that I have struggled for, and the independence of which I cherish, perhaps inordinately.

I am slightly chagrined—but more delighted by the Jungian synchronicity—that an astute English artist has already observed in me limitations I only today perceived for myself. In a letter from London received this afternoon, Anne Buchanan Crosby writes:

I hope you are looking forward to Paris. I am sure you will find it a revelation to be in Europe—you will recognize so many sources of your thinking and so many things will become clear to you—an order that you already have will be made much less of a burden. I mean you will not feel you have to cultivate your understanding of culture. Here is the order made, understood and used everyday. You will just share it. I may not have made a good illustration of what I mean, but I find Americans often carry a heavy burden or at least a lonely one—in their feeling for art—and they simply cannot connect and feel part of a stream. It makes them prima donna-ish at times or it makes them into missionaries carrying a message—which here needs no statement.

21 JANUARY

A day of excitement. Plans changed, I leave my house tomorrow at three P.M., fly to New York and thence directly to Paris, arriving, Deo volente, at eight-thirty on Tuesday morning. Alexandra, who is using a recent legacy to join me in Paris, is already there. I telephoned her to tell her I am coming sooner than we thought. Sleepy-voiced, she said she had just turned out her light, was all cozied in, and would have croissants and coffee for me when I arrived. Then, "Oh, no, we will go out. It's *beautiful* here!"

24 JANUARY

HOTEL DE L'UNIVERSITÉ
22 RUE DE L'UNIVERSITÉ
PARIS, FRANCE

I left my house at three on Sunday afternoon, arrived at the Charles de Gaulle airport in Paris at eight Monday morning, and awoke here in the Latin Quarter at eight this morning, Tuesday, between closely woven cotton sheets under fleecy woolen blankets, as if returned with my grown-up mind to my childhood satisfaction with the world's good providence. In the bed next to mine Alexandra sleeps on while I stretch and look around.

Behind the carved shining wooden doors of a commodious chest, our clothes hang neatly; under them are our suitcases; beside them on shelves, our shoes and oddments. A dresser with ample drawers, a fireplace, a stuffed sofa and armchairs, and a round table covered with a round stout cotton cloth stiffly ironed so that the folds meet at the exact center point, set with two round-backed chairs placed precisely face to face. Two ceiling-high windows with translucent white curtains, and tan draperies drawn for sleep. Every color is a shade of brown, from polished mahogany to the hearts of leaved-pineapples marching in well-spaced stripes up and down the walls. Unspeakably satisfying to an anxious mind like mine that finds the world stubbornly disorderly.

Le petit déjeuner arrives at our door on a round tray: fresh orange juice, coffee with hot milk, lots of different crisp and soft breads, cheese, three kinds of jam. Alexandra wakes up and we sit happily facing each another at our round table. "Sensible" is Alexandra's adjective for the French.

So I too have felt since touching French ground twenty-four hours ago. Intent on my first glimpse of the soil of France, I had been craning out my window for some time before landing, wondering why there was so little light and gradually figuring out that we were coming down in impenetrable fog. So my first sight was the runway on which we were landing: the passengers burst into spontaneous applause, part relief, part admiration for our pilot's skill. Within a few minutes, I was balancing on a rapidly moving belt that ran rather steeply down and up and down to the place of baggage dispersal. Over our heads at a comfortable height a pebbled-concrete vault; glimpses of a great skylight off to the left hinted at sky. An implicit criticism of the John F. Kennedy airport in New York where I had tramped for long minutes in and out of freezing air from one awkward terminal to another, confused by messy organization. Directed by three volubly helpful French people, I found a taxi which bore me to Alexandra by way of the Boulevard Malesherbes to the Place de la Concorde, the Tuileries Gardens, and the Louvre: a space conceived on the level of a grand linear dream underwritten by power into reality. An American voice in me remarked coolly, even as I marveled, "Now I understand the French Revolution; it's *wrong* for any human being to have had this much power." But all that was really none of my business now and I stretched my eyes as I have never stretched them before in human-made space.

I have hitherto felt this kind of satisfaction only in spaces entirely without human presence, in the empty reaches of the American and Australian continents and of the Pacific Ocean; or in great works of art ordered by a scale that felt to me as if it referred to a divine context beyond the human, within which everything human fell into a proper proportion. The architectural space of Paris is an astonishment to me; because its scale so accurately attunes inhabited earth to sky that I can actually walk in a work of art. I feel in some subtle way eased. I find myself in a world ordered by people of like mind to my own, in a companionship rendered visible. As if for the first time in my life I could be content to be human without having to forego, because of that limitation, my intuition of divine order.

25 JANUARY

I do not understand what there is about me that the French instantly and unequivocally identify as American. Alexandra fits into the city like a jigsaw puzzle piece; men and women look at her with a lively appreciation that instantly grants her her place in their intelligent pursuit of their own well-thought-out ends. Even when it is apparent that she speaks no French, she and the Parisians get on a footing right away. They treat me with calibrated politeness, as if I stood at a distinct distance. I feel their curiosity as if I were being examined by the antennae of beings who customarily spend a millisecond summing up as accurately as they can whatever they encounter. They paste the label "American" on my chest and dismiss me with dispatch. This hurts my feelings, even though what they are perceiving is the truth:

I am American and I am irrelevant to their lives.

Last night Alexandra went out to swim and eat with a friend. I asked Madame at the hotel desk for the name of a "neighborhood family restaurant." Her black eyes snapped with the pleasure of giving out apt information. With perfect trust in her common sense, I wound my long blue scarf around my neck and walked off a couple of blocks down the curving street to Julien et Petit. I saw the sign hanging out on high but had passed it before I took it in, and had to turn back to three symmetrical rectangular, anonymously-white-curtained windows, the center one of which I picked out as a door. I lifted an old-fashioned metal latch and entered a long narrow room with four tables each seating four, set on either side of an aisle leading to a desk with flowers on it curving off at the end; a kitchen beyond. The eyes of five diners instantly focused on me with un-abashed objectivity. Madame, a plain stout woman strapped into a grass-green embroidered apron attached, with two safety pins, to her matter-of-fact bosom approached, said "Bien sûr" I could have supper, and waved me to a seat. The menu was as closely written as a laundry list. My French is not up to much explanation. I ordered bean soup, tomato salad, and what I thought Madame would understand as whatever vegetables she had, assembled on a plate. She brought me a napkin, a fork, a knife, and a spoon fit for the mouth of a giantess. A plate of bread, another of sliced tomatoes in oil-and-vinegar dressing with parsley cut up on top, and a bowl of soup. Delectable soup. I asked for an-other bowl but was too shy to ask for butter. By this time Madame and I were at a standoff: she was my hostess and wished to make me feel at home; I was her guest and wished to give her the satisfaction of making me at home. Beneath this, we both wished to do our duty. We gave up words. I ate my bowls of soup with my gigantic spoon and then my plate of tomatoes, and then I asked for *l'addition,* paid fifty francs, and stood up. Very deliberately, I rewound my blue scarf and put on my mittens. Madame and I bade each other a good evening with mutual relief that we had met with dignity our appropriate obligations. I glanced back on my way out the door and saw a young man's sleek head pop out of the kitchen beyond the desk, eyes alive with curiosity over his black mustache.

26 JANUARY

When the light fades on winter afternoons, I am accustomed to feeling sad, as if some will to adjust to the world were seeping out of me. I do not feel this in Paris. Instead, I have the impression that every single Parisian has lived the departing day with as much common sense as possible in a situation that has been thoroughly understood as less than ideal but entirely real; furthermore, that every Parisian expects to make the same effort the following day, and the day following that, without having to reexamine this situation and reinvent a context in which each effort has a meaning above and beyond the day's course. A due and proper sense of what it is to have been born a human being can, it feels to me for the first time in my life, be taken for granted. This enables me to feel that I can easily meet the obligation of being human, and this surprises me, as I am accustomed to an unnerving atmosphere of thought. If the aim of being human is to align oneself with mysterious divine forces informing the world, each moment of life is an effort pragmatically foredoomed to fall short.

In the Cluny Museum yesterday, I stood astounded among the sculptured faces of people who had left behind them evidence that their vital efforts in the thirteenth century had not been in vain because they spoke to me of comfort. The faces of people who had struggled as hard as they could to be good and had had, at last, to accept their own humanity, not as a fatal limitation but as an available form of nobility. They gave me to understand that the effort of a human life can only be this acceptance, a submission to limitations that admit, include, the human virtues as worthy of proportionate divine recognition. I have made a mistake in not paying proper attention to the story of human history. The Cluny faces report that to be human can be what, and all, God expects of us.

Perhaps for this reason, I feel here in Paris that human beings have made a world for themselves to which I can adjust without the distress of habitual alienation. But more than that, with contentment. The simple kind of contentment I have hitherto only experienced with singular people in mutual love and acceptance. For the first time, I understand with my heart why and how social fabric can sustain an individual.

Within this context, art seems to come into due proportion, to have the innocence it has for me in my studio. Perhaps because here I find it where it feels to me it belongs: in churches. And I can *stand inside* it. St. Séverin, the first of the churches Alexandra and I entered yesterday, *included* me, on ground chosen in the sixth century by the hermit Séverin as a place to live out his life with God; under my feet were his feet. In St.-Julien-le-Pauvre, I knelt. Outside me, around me, as if permeating me, an air in which I felt at home. I was absorbed into a reality I have hitherto known only when alone.

So sustained, with the promise of return to this magnetic point, I withstood the contraption of the Beaubourg, an assault, an affront on the senses that seemed, in my mood, quintessentially all that I eschew. Alexandra and I grasped the railing of the escalator that snakes up the western facade and launched ourselves onto a roof platform from which we viewed Paris as if from one of those rickety ladders off which circus acrobats dive into tiny tanks. We did not (I regret) enter the museum, but made our way, map clutched in our chilled hands, to the Louvre.

The Louvre rolled up a lifetime's study of art into a pellet and spat it out in my ignorant face. Screams of terror overlaid by screams for blood echoed through corridors dimensionless as those in nightmares, ironically lined with art of such authority that I stood as much aghast as dazzled.

Whenever I have seen art in its land of origin, I have been struck by its reliance on place. In America Japanese art looks withdrawn into itself, as if stiffened in what might poetically be thought of as self-defense; Australian Aboriginal art, unutterably powerful in Australia, loses meaning, can even look childish, decorative, when carted off that continent, losing force as visibly as a rainbow trout fades when cast onto the bank of a river. The European art I have seen in America seems anemic in comparison to what I am seeing here. I sometimes wish that photography were solely in the hands of artists who photograph rather than a tool so commonly used for the reproduction of images. Reproduction fatally weakens the force of art, reducing its presence to mere information and thus rendering it accessible in a way that makes it easy to miss the point of it.

By the time we had stood beneath the *Victory of Samothrace,* before the *Venus de Milo,* the *Mona Lisa*—among other masterpieces—and entered the gallery of nineteenth-century French painting, both Alexandra and I were flushed with exhilaration. The translucent green wave on the left of

Géricault's *The Raft of the Medusa* swelled out of this sea of feeling. Delacroix's paintings met it and bore me aloft to restore me to my modern eye, my accustomed focus on art. A focus I observe to be merely serviceable in a vision now as abruptly in transition as that from a plane rising swiftly into the air.

Today we go to Chartres by tour bus.

We went to our bus at the Place des Pyramides on the rue de Rivoli by way of the Place de l'Opéra. I stood and gazed around and up at the Opéra and felt like a brick, awkward in my ugly woolen cap bought for warmth and the stout leather rubber-soled shoes in which I walk the halls of the University of Maryland and my indestructible tweed coat. Actually, I started to faint (partly jet lag) and Alexandra hurried me into a cafe for hot soup. In one of those dream-like sequences in which the enchanting without warning begins to dissolve into the macabre, Paris turned cold as a serpent's scales. I could see how beautiful it was, how opulent in ornament, how grand in the achievements of its people, how amusing, how quintessentially civilized, but chill remained.

Hot soup and coffee and a delectable little lemon tart helped, but something had been lost, as if I had fallen out of love with a man I had adored, not unwisely perhaps, but too quickly. The bus was soothing—the passivity—and I noted the names of the streets on our way out of Paris with renewed, if subdued, enthusiasm: rue La Fontaine, rue Gros, rue George Sand, rue Poussin, rue Girodet, rue Géricault. A declaration of formidable French achievement on the Parisian gray cream walls that slowly gave way to a countryside patched with snow against earth drenched umber. Light dwelt among the twigged branches of the trees, here wild, there cut to the shape of flowers on stalks. Either the color key of France is naturally perfect, acutely and accurately unified in all its infinite inflections of tone and hue, or my eye has been trained by paintings of it to recognize this kind of keyed unity as the essence of the art of painting. I kept thinking that I could simply *copy* what I was seeing and I would have what would be instantly recognizable as a painting.

We paused at Versailles to pick up new passengers. Alexandra and I, seated at windows across from one another, raised our eyebrows at one another to exclaim silently across the bus aisle at its magnificence. Leaving Versailles, we passed by the stables that Louis XIV commissioned Jules Hardouin-Mansard to design for his 2500 horses. The cool American voice in me that had noted the Place de la Concorde as out of moral proportion spoke again, this time in no uncertain terms. Hungry people and coddled horses—no. I mounted the barricades of the *Révolution* and have not since deserted them. With similar conviction, my Puritan forebears departed from England for Massachusetts in 1634.

Self-righteousness faded rapidly as we rolled on into the Beauce countryside. Moss grew richly in the crevices of the ancient stone walls around the Rambouillet forest. The smooth, slow-sloping plowed fields beyond were a tender rose color like the inside of a ripe fig, graced by patches of woods, a deep dark brown curiously laced with raspberry. Occasionally the cluster of a farm, close to the ground, mottled inextricably earth and stone; and little towns, set apart from their encircling fields, each steepled above motley slanted roofs. Then, way off beyond in the soft air above empty fields, I saw the spires of Chartres, dwelling on the land, at home: *le bon Dieu.*

Of all the legacies left me by my parents, the habit of reverence stretches furthest back in my memory and has lasted as most nourishing. At Chartres I saw reverence rendered visible, and there my pilgrim spirit came to rest.

28 JANUARY

Alexandra just left for Orly Airport. We hugged good-bye with difficult smiles. Now I am alone in Paris in a smaller room under the eaves of our hotel. I am so high up in this attic that all I can see out my narrow windows is a gray mansard roof across the street. Above it the sky is the very definition of gray.

29 JANUARY

A vegetarian who does not drink wine is at a loss in France. On the other hand, the impersonality of the French embraces all eccentricity. On Alexandra's sound advice, I have stopped trying to explain myself and simply order my solitary bits and pieces of food. Madame can do no wrong. My francs entirely meet my obligation. This morning I awoke to the sound of rain on the roof right over my head. I will clasp my umbrella firmly and tramp out to St.-Julien-le-Pauvre, out and back along the Boulevard St. Germain, staying on Alexandra's and my familiar tracks. Will have a nap today. A restless night last night. I am lonely.

In 1979 Mary went to France alone for her junior year at Sarah Lawrence College. By mishappenchance, she was neither met nor welcomed in any way by the college authorities and she returned home within a few days. I disagreed with her decision, though I honored it as it is my habit to do with my children's decisions since they reached young adulthood. I understood that the adjustment was honestly beyond her capacity. But I never understood why until today. French matter-of-factness has the fault of its virtue: it seems so to separate fact from feeling that it compounds the loneliness of strangers. Isolated from the tenderness that must lie somewhere within the rational way in which the French confront life, a visitor is forced to adjust without the amenities of hospitality.

One of the reasons I had been so confident that Mary would be able to find her way in Paris was her experience in Japan, where we lived for almost four years of her childhood. I had assumed that the French culture, from which ours is partially derived, would be even easier for her to fit into, but I now realize that the Japanese, while never for a moment forgetting to draw a line between themselves and foreigners, have so developed ways and means of accommodation that they behave *as if* they were welcoming long enough to enable a visitor to adjust to their ways. Poetically speaking, France is a geometric theorem, a forbidding arrangement of fixed blocks; Japan is an air, its natives having developed intuition to such a high degree under the pressure of crowding that it animates their system of polite formulae.

30 JANUARY

I was so paralyzed by loneliness yesterday morning that I could do nothing. Dozed and read and lunched in my room. Then, forgetting my umbrella in my general rout, walked over to the church of St.-Germain-des-Prés, where I sat numbly and listened to organ music. On to St. Sulpice, to

Delacroix's last two grand paintings: *Heliodorus in the Temple* and *Jacob Wrestling with the Angel.*

Jacob *wrestles* with the Angel. He can do no more. He has dropped his accoutrements on the ground behind him. Every muscle is distended. The Angel is simply of another, infinitely stronger, order. They engage one another on a hill in the foreground of the painting. Behind and below them and beyond into the distance wind Jacob's people. They are not called upon to struggle; they handle routine affairs, organize the horses and the baggage train. Only Jacob is set apart to engage another realm, to risk fall—and to be blessed. Above, a great tree unifies them all, rising aloof in the sun to which the earth owes its visibility. The painting is deep in color, powerful in stroke, but as I sat on a little straight wooden chair in my wet coat looking up into it I understood all the sad inevitability of death.

3 1   J A N U A R Y

Time is the protagonist of Europe. The cloth on which I have imprinted my conceptualizations of life is too short. Of stout American cotton, it resists the stretching to which it is being subjected and I am being psychically elasticized—not torn—on a rack I never knew existed. I wish for Henry James to sit beside me in his splendidly tailored bulk, and explain; I can see why Daisy Miller grew fevered and simply died; I would like to have tea with Ralph Touchett.

In the Place Vendôme yesterday, I imagined my work face to face with its elegant façades and felt for the first time the full force of Clement Greenberg's statement that in my sculpture I had "flirted with the look of non-art."* A few

*Vogue, May 1968.

wooden boards painted white. Could they be art at all? In the beginning, in 1961, I never thought about that. I walked on the open airy fields of my own mind among the sculptures I was making and intended to make without ever looking beyond my own entirely engrossing world. I had no idea that I was being daring.

In the pantheon of artists whose work I am seeing, I draw closer to Van Gogh. He hangs next to Gauguin in the Jeu de Paume and when I saw them together I suddenly knew why Gauguin so disappointed him in his yearning for an ideal companionship with a fellow artist. Gauguin was attracted by wickedness, but failed to grasp the terrible reality of evil. This is a critical distinction between people. No deeply serious relationship is possible without congruence on this critical point. People who know that evil exists do not play with wickedness, as Gauguin seems to me to do in his painting—references to spirits good and bad, ghostly inferences that hover. Van Gogh's insight is relentless. No matter what the literal subject matter of his paintings, their content, implicit in brushstroke and color, is the interpenetration of good and evil rendered transcendent by way of his art.

2   FEBRUARY

I leave Paris this evening from the Gare de Lyon for Padua, where my Danish friend, Annelise Seidenfaden, will meet me early tomorrow morning.

Henry James remains the person with whom I wish desperately to speak. Even to sit next to, to feel his American intelligence vibrating inside him. Europe is an immeasurable shock to me. More even than Japan, partly because of the Japanese affinity for amenity and partly because I was less vulnerable when I landed there, armored by a good opinion of myself and ordered by the imperative demands of a husband who was not well and three young children.

Last night I went out to a dinner. Even though the conversation was largely in rapid, colloquial French which I could neither understand nor respond to adequately, I was infinitely soothed by impeccable conventionality. The whole evening was so familiar: the candlelit rooms, the abundant flowers, the elegant clothes, the responsive exchanges, the atmosphere of pleasure to be given and taken in ease. For the first time since Alexandra left Paris, I relaxed. So when the Englishman on my right at dinner began to speak in witty disparagement of a James Truitt whom he had met in Mexico through their mutual interest in pre-Columbian archeology, I was totally taken by surprise. Our hostess intervened. When this gentleman grasped my relationship to James Truitt, he put his hand on my arm gently and said, "I'm sorry." I sat perfectly straight but I felt shot, as if the bullet with which James had killed himself had pierced my breast.

The artist in me is the only part of me who has *not* succumbed to all the tides, personal and impersonal, of this trip. She is shocked but rises resiliently to each shock with the fierce conviction that she never before has had strong enough food.

Of course Cézanne's *La Femme Etranglée* and *La Madelaine à la Douleur* had, logically, to precede the perfection of his achieved balance. And the great *Baigneurs* echo off that passion drawn through the experience of a master. Renoir's late canvases, particularly *Les Baigneuses,* are a revelation of an incomparable sensuousness impossible to grasp in reproduction; as if the physical, allowed its full glory, can lead the way to an inevitable dissolution at once earthly and unearthly. Monet's utter mastery of atmosphere is akin to my own preoccupation with color as a form of an imminent truth otherwise inaccessible. He achieves it stroke by stroke; I attempt to catch it by way of superimposed films of inflected color. Manet's *Le Déjeuner sur l'Herbe* and *Olympia* are shocking paintings. I felt my bones shake. And now I understand why cubism was invented in France, and *collage:* everything visual here is complexly overlaid, and slivered by the penetration of this particularly lucid light. It demands a new intellectual order to serve its truth, which in turn requires a born-in-the-bone confidence in the power of the intellect to invent such an order. Artists have ever since been dependent on the accuracy and implications of this formulation.

I have just pulled my curtain aside to see the sky—as cold a gray as ever. I draw back inside myself. There I stand on the wide reaches of the American continent, return to dimensionless breadths of land and sky, and in my hand I feel my brush, laden with just enough paint, draw one translucent veil of color over another in stretches to match their latitudes.

I said good-bye to Paris in two places.

Delacroix remains a presence in his studio. I sat humbly on a chair upon which he may perhaps have sat, and quietly thanked him for the companionship of his life. It is this companionship—Delacroix's and that of the other artists whose work I am seeing—that I shall take with me when I leave Europe. The stubborn intransigence of my own nerve, coupled with fierce independence, has made me reluctant to consort with other artists, no matter how wholeheartedly I may be impressed by their achievements. This self-reliance may well be a fault—it certainly has made me lonely—but if so it is one I have earned with every atom of my experience. It penetrates deep within and throughout my character, as proliferated and as intrinsic to my life and movement as the delicately boned skeleton of a fish.

At St.-Julien-le-Pauvre, I lit a candle, and my inarticulate prayer joined those of the folk who for 1500 years and more have raised their silent voices in that place, on that ground. The church sits there plainly, declaring without declamation the fact that Bishop Julien's life exemplified: only by giving away can one receive. The human must relinquish the personal to know the divine.

4 FEBRUARY

LA GUIZZA
ASOLO, ITALY

For all my efforts to be correct, I was in the wrong *couchette* from Paris to Padua: number thirty-eight when my ticket was for number thirty-two. I did not notice until I was on my way out of the train yesterday morning. This was a lucky mistake because my companion in number thirty-eight was an Italian woman on her way home to Trieste from a visit in Paris, and she made the trip happy for me. A plump woman—black hair, black dress, black shoes, as comforting as an experienced nurse. She takes the trip often and she knew the conductor; she spoke French, so I had to speak only French and found that I could quite fluently. We were alone, each on a lower berth. She helped me with the customs declaration and showed me how to make up my berth with a white cotton sack into which she insisted I push my handbag down against my feet so no thief could get at it while I slept. Without ado, she simply lay down in her dress inside her sack, pulled the blanket over her, went to sleep, and snored in the most soothing way. So I slept too, cozily. I awoke once to see out the window a thick slice of Swiss snow that looked like carved marble, but mostly I slept like a protected child. Her good humor was unfathomable. She laughed and chatted as if we were old friends in some way at once personal and impersonal, inhabitants, say, of the same village. We shook hands good-bye with mutual appreciation.

And there at the bottom of the steep iron train steps in Padua was Annelise Seidenfaden, as much her dear self as she was when we had last parted in 1961. This continuity of a healthy human personality is one of the wonders of life to me, the fact that people remain throughout the years so distinctly themselves. In no time, she had bought me a little roll and a cappuccino—a delectable surprise of cooling milk froth and hot, hot strong coffee (not bitter like French coffee), whisked me through the restroom (paying a woman for toilet paper!) into her nifty little car, and out into the Italian countryside, which emerged from the mists of dawn as deliberately as a sequence filmed by a master.

I began to understand almost immediately why Italian painters invented landscape painting: such beauty sings a lyric no artist could resist. By the time we reached Giorgíone's Castelfranco, the sun was up (the first time I had seen it for days) and pressed on the orange-gold ramparts of the old town as if blessing them. But without any of the theatricality that always sets my teeth on edge. There were the walls and there in the tender blue sky was the sun: they met as old friends, easily, as if pleased but not surprised to be together. Rather like Annelise's friends meeting one another in the Caffè Centrale in the square of Asolo, where we had breakfast. Then out to her domain, La Guizza, a series of buildings including Annelise's flourishing ceramics studio and set on a meandering line in gardens backed into a hill overlooking a broad, enticing valley ending to the south in the Euganean hills and to the northwest in the great snow-covered Grappa Mountains that lead to the Alps.

After settling me, we wound along a muddy country road to an ancient farmhouse that Annelise has bought and is lovingly restoring: a house made out of the stones and the woods around it, made right out of what the earth provided. No higher than it need be to enter for shelter, its form is determined by its function in proportions of endearing modesty.

My intuition on my arrival in Paris of the intelligence and comfort of the European way of life has been affirmed by the ease I feel in the company of Annelise and her friends. To an extent, their habits have become my habits. When I heard that the Caffé Centrale closes every Tuesday (today), my heart sank. Annelise laughed when I mentioned it and said, "We meet in another place but we feel the same way." For these meetings give the days an episodic continuity, a pleasant meaning independent of whatever work is done. Like flocks of birds, friends alight in the Caffé early in the morning, at noon before a leisurely lunch of many courses, and in the evening before an even more leisurely late dinner. They are birds on the wing: one second everyone is chatting away as if they had all the time in the world, the next they are all immediately aflight, with none of the ritual reassurances with which I am accustomed to part politely from people because they all understand that they will be meeting again in a few hours. Whatever threads they drop, they simply pick up again. In Tokyo, feet clopped in *geta,* wooden platforms along which the foot was held rigid, aloof from mud; in Paris, I soon came to recognize the smart tap of women's heels as a heartbeat of the city. Here in Italy, people alight and take off in flight all sound and gesture to me, as I neither speak nor understand Italian.

In Paris, I recognized a commonality founded on a social structure I could only infer, but here in Asolo I am enveloped without ceremony in gesticulations so lively and eloquent that I am included. I am fascinated by a balance of community and work that makes life comfortable in a way entirely new to me. Because they meet so frequently and regularly throughout the course of a day, Annelise's friends weave among them a texture of interchange that includes the details of their lives, each only a few hours old so their communication is fresh from meeting to meeting. They discuss (Annelise translates for me) everything that they do, embroidering it all with the immediacy of their reactions. This leaves no time for misunderstanding to foliate. They are always busy explaining themselves to one another with the kind of exhaustive coziness I have observed only in congenial southern families in the United States.

Their work punctuates these meetings, as if it were the warp and woof of their community with each other, providing the structure of their days as well as many of the details they exchange. The proportion of work to converse is close to fifty-fifty, in sharp contrast to the American separation of the day into mutually exclusive periods of work and relaxation, work taking up most of the day and relaxation constituting a compensatory reward for effort. It occurs to me that marriages may stand a better chance of happiness in these conditions. If the husband comes home at noon for a hot dinner followed by a rest, he and his wife so nearly share each day's events that they could, I speculate, come to sympathize with the contexts of one another's lives in an ordinary way, unweighted by the artificial drama of parting in the morning and re-meeting in the evening.

These reflections on the closely woven texture of social life here were echoed this morning when after our cappuccino Annelise took me to see a distinguished Asolo silk weaver. A woman whose face is the unadorned record of a life of devotion, as pure as that of a saint.

Silkworms apparently have to *learn* how to spin their cocoons; the early reaches of the thread are coarse, and the last also as the worm's energies decrease; only the central threads are fine and even. Over the years, the worms have been bred to spin a whiter and whiter thread, more easily dyed; I was shown a hank of what they spun before these genetic changes took effect: the strands were as golden as Rapunzel's hair. At the end of a long, dusty dark hall, I saw a cloud of steam rising over a huge iron vat in which the raw silk hanks hung on a rack. The vat was set casually over a fagot fire in a cramped alcove off a tangled garden. This boiling process eliminates one third of the diameter of the thread, that part which is the worm's saliva. After being dyed, the thread is carried up a flight of splintered stairs to be woven in a room full of very old wooden looms attended by women who sit silent at their weaving in a deafening *clack-clack-clack,* as if in fairy thrall. A little mirror attached by a nail to a post supporting the attic ceiling ties them to womankind: a rectangular mirror above a narrow shelf on which lay a comb full of black hairs. The thought flashed across my mind that this assemblage was the sort that I had been seeing in art galleries for years; but not akin, as this mirror was for use and the hairs were these women's homely combings alike to the threads of the silkworms that before my eyes were becoming cloth by way of fire, water, color, and human hands. The father of Saint Francis must have managed his skeins just so.

This afternoon we drove to Bassano, a town near Asolo. It lies along a high curving ridge overlooking the Grappa Mountains, bordered on the edge of this ridge by a broad low wall. This wall is in turn lined by a series of trees with straight trunks and round foliage, and on each there is a nameplate and a metal basket. A few weeks before the end of the Second World War, the Germans caught the young members of a resistance group and immediately hanged every single person, one to each tree. There are artificial flowers in all the baskets; in one, a fresh branch of pussy willow just fuzzing with the coming spring. A few blocks away, an intricately stressed wooden bridge like ancient ones in Japan stretches across the river that winds through the town; it was over this bridge that Napoleon entered Bassano in conquest. The walls lining the river on one side of the bridge are pockmarked with the now-mossy holes made by his cannonballs.

I stood quietly on this bridge for a while and watched the slow river eddy. Our lives move along, bearing our past into our future.

9 FEBRUARY

When Annelise and I entered Venice yesterday, I remembered Mary McCarthy's dictum that everything that anyone could ever say about Venice someone has already said. No wonder. Only the mute could resist exclamation!

The Academia was closed, and the Doge's Palace too—a strike of some sort, wherever we went ornate doors stood shut in the wintry wind. So it is not the art that I had hoped to see that I have brought away with me from Venice but the memory of the golden particles that under the dome of San Marco seemed to me to hold in glorious suspension the sound of a magnificent bell. That, and the startling pure green of the Adriatic Sea. In the glittering resonance under the cathedral dome, within the encircling arm of that lovely sea, I felt a splendor in the human spirit so real that within it any individual death—my own, for example—was subsumed. This—the intensity of this beauty—would continue to be, and that was enough to know. Though there was more. Faith was illuminated, irradiated, encompassing all equally, so that I stood as if protected under the spread of infinitely wide and beneficent wings.

The rest was all the pleasures that incident provides imagination: unusual proximities, fetching vistas, details of wet and dry stone, reflections of water, bandit cats.

Annelise's farmhouse has been roofed. Last night we met at a country inn to celebrate, for when a roof is finished here branches are raised above it and all the people connected with the house—owner, architect, workmen—meet to feast. The branches over Annelise's roof, chosen by one of the younger workmen, hark poetically to the old and the new: a great bunch of the vines that had covered the house for unnumbered years and a Botticelli-like young tree, graceful branches alight with the tiny, pale yellow leaves of the coming spring.

The man who last night sat on my right at the long narrow table is the foreman of the group of artisans. He speaks neither English nor French, so our companionship was silent but nonetheless eloquent, for I felt as if I knew him because the other day I had watched him (and he had noticed me watching) cementing the rocks on the interior walls of the old farmhouse: a skillful slap of grout, then patient scraping, then water so the stones stood clear. This deliberate attention to process is familiar to me in the work I have done in sculpture—I made life-size human figures in colored cement during the 1950s—and I felt at home with him in a sense almost intimate. I felt his body beside mine, a solid personification of values I share with him, for he bears not only the dignity of years of painstaking labor but also of responsibility. He is the master craftsman. One of the celebrating workmen is his apprentice, only sixteen: a serious boy on his way to becoming a serious man.

Course followed course for some hours. On either side of me, up and down the table, I saw faces familiar to me only in art. I was dining with Etruscans, with Romans.

Content to be a minor figure in this frieze, I recalled the Villa Maser, which Annelise and I visited last Sunday. Originally the Villa Barbaro, its elegance, wrought by the hands of men like my companions, was Palladio's conception, as grand as Annelise's farmhouse is humble. It rises atop a hill and dominates the land around it as the Barbaro family must have dominated sixteenth-century Italian society.

The present owners are Annelise's friends, so I had the moving experience of seeing it both as glorious architecture and as home. Like the branches waving on Annelise's roof, the new is being tactfully folded into the old. We Americans have no such mellow grandeur. There is no way, except by an imaginative empathy inevitably awry, that I can grasp in its entirety the proud tenderness the Italians feel for their past.

As in Bassano, I am impressed by the weaving of the past into the present, by the inclusion of history in the everyday consciousness of people. At the Villa Maser, this inclusion is by way of art so that history is not only preserved but transcended, raised above the depredations of time. Marcel Proust was able to achieve this by his special attentiveness to his life, by his recognition that certain moments of his experience were, by virtue of their ecstatic quality, preserved in his memory intact in all their freshness. Artists in an analogous way preserve the high points of human history, intellectual and spiritual insights they pass down to posterity in art as vivid as reactivated memory.

I O F E B R U A R Y

In 1300 Enrico Scrovegni bought the land in Padua on which the Roman Amphitheater of Patavium had stood since A.D. 60. Inside the area of the Arena, he built a chapel in which around 1305 Giotto painted the Christian story of the Redemption of Man, from the Conception of the Virgin Mary to the Pentecost after Christ's Ascension. The paintings are an encircling series of frescoes, three tiers reading from left to right, then left again, top to bottom, the whole panorama culminating in an immense Last Judgment that spans the wall above the door. The chapel is a forthright rectangle. I felt immediately that in so plain a structure I could trust that the inside walls would match the outside: a statement without equivocation, in line with my native sensibility.

I stepped over the threshold into a world I had so long inhabited in my imagination that I felt it would feel familiar.

Instead, I was brought to a standstill by utter astonishment: a reality breathtakingly beyond any imagining. Transfixed, I followed the sequence from one panel to another as if Giotto had just put down his brush and left a message for me to read; a message in which he had so densely combined the divine with the human that they explained and illuminated one another as they are meant to do in our lives. The logic of the explanation depends here in this chapel on a stretch of imagination, as the validity of the premise cannot be verified. This premise being that the divine can so penetrate the human as to create a new life without recourse to the physical interaction of father and mother. Logic dictates that purity can emerge only out of purity, demands that the conception of Christ be divinely initiated. This premise stuck in my craw for a long while when I was younger, but my lifetime has often required me to believe the unbelievable and I am prepared to hold all and any ideas as working hypotheses. Also, when I had, like Saint Anne, difficulty in conceiving a child, I came to realize conception to be a divine act; that contraception is within our scientific control blinds us to this fact. However details may be, the penetration of the divine into the human is a fundamental truth that life has taught me and teaches me each successive day. So my experience echoes Giotto's piety.

But piety is relatively common. Consummate art is not, nor is wise humanness, and the intensity of my response to Giotto's painting arose out of my recognition that he had been able by way of supreme art to render visible the confrontation of what he had experienced as evil in human beings with what he had experienced as good, and to render them justly, so that this range of experience had meaning within the illumination of the transcendental. Over and over again, my heart was caught by his wisdom and tenderness. The dignity of Joachim and Anne in their childlessness, the delicacy with which Anne bestows upon Joachim the kiss that symbolizes the conception of the Virgin Mary; the eagerness with which she reaches for her newborn daughter, to be eloquently refracted later in the complementary gesture of renunciation with which Mary gives over her baby son to the priest in the temple, to the life and death she knows lie before Him; the eloquent look Christ gives His mother, and she Him, as He starts on the road to Calvary bearing the cross on which He is to be crucified. I was brought up in the Christian church but this is in no way the reason for these responses, which have their source in my own life: the joy of first holding my children in my arms, the discipline with which I have been, as all parents are, forced to acquiesce to their suffering, and, finally, the recognition that for all that my children do not *belong* to me, they and I are joined in an indissoluble human bond.

The coupling of Giotto's profoundly empathetic understanding with his technical mastery of art is what makes his work so important to me. I have become accustomed to seeing technical mastery used either in its own service in a declamatory way, or in explorations of the nature of visual perception, or psychological apperception. Rarely, never so forcefully and so ardently, in an attempt to illuminate the whole of the human relationship with the divine in so many ramifications of innuendo and event.

I had always been made uneasy by the rocks in Giotto's landscapes, harsh and cold in reproductions. In reality, their grays are marvelously inflected, sympathetic to the eye, paradigmatically natural because they offset the architecture of the buildings in the frescoes. The two little trompe l'oeil paintings of chapel interiors that flank the chancel arch were also revelations. I have never seen them reproduced and was astonished by their delicate, fresh color, by their skillful perspective and most of all by their implicit declaration of "art for art's sake." To my eye, they are critical to the entire chapel, not only because they reenforce the union of the paintings with their architectural setting, thus locking art into the physical, but also because they claim, unequivocally but without flourish, a validity for art in itself. They adumbrate the values I take for granted, the values that mysteriously reside in form—formal values.

MONTE   SAN   SAVINO

The deep sleep of last night wove around me an intricate filigree of pale green vines that slowly became transparent and dissolved, leaving me in a limpid space, but alone, with tears in my eyes and grief that James was not at my side. So many times I woke and turned to him for continuity in strange, new places while we were traveling. Deep inside other reasons for missing his presence in my life, a kernel does not dissolve: the loss of continuity. The interwoven animation of the French and, more vividly, the Italians, has shelled me and this kernel is exposed.

I must be my own continuity. I have to keep on spinning it out of myself, in my life and in my work. Sleep spun it for me last night, and gave me, like a friendly husband, understanding this morning.

Yesterday afternoon Annelise and I drove here to Monte San Savino for a visit to Tuscany: west from Asolo, across and down the peninsula of Italy to this little town spiraled atop a conical Tuscan hill.

Tuscany is a land after some secret part of my heart, sensuous as a woman inside her own body. The bones are explicit in its undulating contours, and even in winter the earth luxuriates over them as if warmed from within. Nothing the human eye would want is missing. Variety dwells serenely as if each detail were a perfect part of verity.

Today we go to Sansepolcro and Arezzo, on the trail of Piero della Francesca's paintings.

The streets of Sansepolcro, Piero's native town, are narrow, lined with ancient buildings that cut and slice the sky into a pattern of dark against light, abstractions of proportions and lines of force I recognized with surprise as those of my own work. We went straight to the civic museum and there I saw them in the spatial construction of Piero's paintings.

His *Madonna della Misericordia,* the *Virgin of Mercy,* stands straight in a long, lightly girdled reddish-pink gown over which she wears a full dark blue cloak lined with pale brown. Her arms are outstretched and under them cluster eight figures so reduced in scale that their heads only reach her knees. They kneel in individualized, characteristic attitudes of adoration. The Virgin's eyes are lowered under heavy lids as if she were blessing them from a remote spiritual distance reenforced by the strong pillar of her perfect neck. I was absolutely fascinated by the tilts off the vertical and horizontal that endow the painting with visual life. The major panel of a polyptych, its vertical dimension rises up just off the center of the Virgin's body into the smaller panel of the Crucifixion above her head, in which the cross is again slightly displaced off center. The arms of the cross extend straight on the horizontal, but again not quite evenly so that the balance between their very slightly different lengths and the Virgin's open arms, which are in turn of different lengths as well as being tilted off the horizontal, enlivens the space of the painting as breath mysteriously and ever newly enlivens a body.

Piero's *Resurrection* hangs directly opposite this painting. Against tenderly articulated Tuscan hills, trees, and a luminescent sky, the magnificent figure of the risen Christ commands His own tomb by placing His foot firmly upon its stone rampart. Below, four figures spraddled in unconsciousness are coarse by comparison, but in no way deprived of justice: their sleep is that of human exhaustion. Nature, human nature, and the divine—embodied in a man who is at once entirely experienced in everything that a person can know of the good and evil of the world and above its power further to instruct—are all juxtaposed in a parable about the potential inherent in consciousness.

A statue of Piero della Francesca himself overlooks his house in Sansepolcro and the hills of Tuscany. Under my feet I trod the very stones on which he must have walked. Later in the day in the church of San Francesco, Arezzo, I humbly recognized in a background view of Jerusalem in *Legend of the True Cross* the direct line between Piero and my debt to him: towers of color. I saw them first in a lecture on Italian painting at Bryn Mawr. They must have stamped themselves into my eye and imagination, to emerge years later, each isolated as I myself had been isolated, thrusting up in a different air in a different place, rising from a different motivation, but out of a sensitivity aligned to Piero's. As I turn this over in my mind, remembering on the soles of my feet the stoned streets of Sansepolcro and in the sky the cut interstices of its buildings, and juxtaposing them with the solitary verticals on the horizontal marshes of my childhood, the way of an artist becomes less lonely. The community of artists, greater and lesser as their gifts decree, can be lived in as an atmosphere, nourishing as air.

Piero's *Madonna del Parto* is in the chapel of the cemetery at Monterchi, where his mother was born. We wound up a little hill to this chapel through a narrow lane lined with pointed cypress. As we stood waiting for the caretaker to let us in, I listened to the wind in the trees with an exalted feeling of union with everything around me; as if, for once, all conflict had been disarmed. The *Madonna* is for me the most moving of all Piero's paintings. She stands alone be-tween heavy embroidered curtains drawn by small attend-ant angels on either side. In a homely gesture, she is open-ing her gown with her hand so that she may more distinctly detect the first pangs of her labor, of the parting of her baby from her body. On her face, the seriousness that is the universal hallmark of motherhood.

The Uffizi Museum in Florence closes on Sunday at one o'clock so we had on our arrival from Monte San Savino only one and a half hours there. Taxed, I had to choose carefully which paintings to look at, each one an overlay of what it was in reality on what I had for years imagined it to be. Uccello's color astonished me, solemn. Botticelli, less a surprise than a confirmation. Caravaggio, overwhelmingly more compelling than I had ever thought him. Rubens, as tight as I had hoped he would be, an uncompromising, austere eye in the service of an exuberant sensibility. Leo-nardo—but I find I cannot write. It is as if I had been released into a grand roll of thunder that makes words sound tinny. Better to leave it reverberating in my memory. Now a memory trued by reality.

We tracked Masaccio to the church of Santa Maria

Novella, and to the Brancacci Chapel in Santa Maria del Carmine. His *Expulsion from Paradise* has haunted me for years: just so, violently, does guilt slice innocence—irrevocably. Tears are no use after a deed is done. But Masaccio's *Adam and Eve* come to their death under Piero's hand in his frescoes at San Francesco in Arezzo. From Adam's ancient flesh springs the Tree of Knowledge, later to furnish the wood for Christ's cross, so that out of his bones rises a means of redemption, as surely as spiritual growth rises out of the responsible acceptance of fault. Now that I am growing old, I can look with clear eyes on Eve's life, from Eden to her grave. In Piero's painting, she stands like a tree herself on her still solid legs, her hand on the bone of Adam's shoulder; her breasts hang in folds of worn flesh: they have fed many; honor lends them grace.

We left Florence at twilight and, by chance, stopped for dinner at San Giovanni Voldarno, Masaccio's birthplace. By that time we were spent. We returned to Asolo this morning.

The accidents of travel are peremptory. Florence yesterday was in large part closed to us, as Venice had been. The Arno River meant less to me than I had thought it would. When I looked at its swift shimmer, I thought of Romula's wicked Tito, of his body borne off like a bundle of rags to catch on snags; George Eliot felt potential violence in its waters and I did too. Florence felt altogether dangerous to me. Its walls were the most powerful I have ever felt in my life, as if they had been saturated with blood and dried out as they stood. But such reactions can be in themselves accidental, the secretions of fatigue, of psychic exhaustion. What remains with me is my astonishment that the reality of art and of all that I am seeing is so beyond what I ever have, or could have, imagined. It is as if I had been entertaining hypotheses restricted to black and white, and have discovered color.

I am sitting in the sun at La Guizza for the last time. Annelise and I fly tonight to London; I leave for Washington two days later.

A postcard that I have used as a bookmark ever since Mary brought it to me from the Jeu de Paume in 1979 lies before me on the desk: Cézanne's *L'Estaque*. A landscape of land and sea and sky in sun contravened by a strip all across the top of the painting that is so dark and deep a blue that it thunders. This card is symbolic of my European trip, as I have now seen the painting with my own eyes and know where the color of the reproduction is wrong and can correct it in my memory. As its scale has incalculably stretched and widened, many details of my inner landscape have become alive.

I am tired now, ready to return to my own land. This morning at breakfast, an Englishwoman who is also Annelise's guest here spoke of a European friend who had married an Englishman and had been unable to adjust to living in England because she was frightened by its being an island; she felt insecure without other countries spread around her to which she could go without crossing a barrier of water. Europeans take abrupt, more or less total, topological and cultural changes for granted. They have a certain superiority in flexibility, a range of interest and experience to which it is difficult for me to adjust, impossible for me to acquire, and silly for me to pretend to. But Europeans might well be dismayed by a drive through the American southwest. I have driven there hour after hour without seeing another human being or evidence of any, and have felt deeply content in the singular meeting of land and sky. The Eastern Shore of Maryland is, like Venice, estuarial. Venice is irresistible, civilization personified, but—and crucially but —its allure is less important to me than the tides that enter and leave it without reference to its existence.

18 FEBRUARY

LONDON, ENGLAND

Nonetheless, the beauty of Venice from the air last night took my breath away: circlets of scintillas set in black velvet. Then, almost immediately, we were flying over the Alps under which about two weeks ago I had been borne by train through the Simplon Tunnel. Snow-covered, the great mounded contours of the earth could be traced by moonlight and by the sparkling necklaces that marked habitations lying along the sinuous lines of the valleys. We flew on over France, a carpet of black splashed with the immense phosphorescent blossoms of anonymous cities, and then, quite suddenly, I saw beneath the plane's wing the coast of England precisely delineated by a narrow glittering rim.

Today we have seen in an exhibit at the Royal Academy, "The Genius of Venice 1500–1600," some of the Venetian art we missed on our strike-stricken visit. Opulent Veroneses and Titians: orchestrations of space and color; Tintoretto's *Pietà,* a painting that is now a rudder for me, rising as it does from a keel of profound honesty to that line between the human and the divine I have been tracing in all the art I have seen during these weeks.

The exhibit of "The Omega Workshops 1913–1919,

Decorative Arts of Bloomsbury," was like a family visit, so familiar are the names of Bloomsbury—Venessa Bell, Roger Fry, Duncan Grant. On to the National Gallery, specifically to see our last three Piero della Francescas: a Saint Michael that Annelise spotted unexpectedly across a gallery, *The Late Nativity,* and *The Baptism of Christ;* a Leonardo cartoon for *Saint Anne, the Virgin, and Child;* Rembrandt; Rubens.

We could do no more. Lowering our eyes, we sped out of the Gallery into a cab in which we drove along Pall Mall to Buckingham Palace (the chatty driver remarked that his wife thought the Queen should keep her curtains whiter) beside St. James's Park where I saw the descendants of the ducks I had fed there with my sisters on a visit to England when I was ten. The Artillery Mansions, where we had taken an apartment for a month, is still there; we drove into the courtyard and I saw the remembered round fountain and forbiddingly close blackened-red brick walls tiered with windows. Behind those windows on one rainy afternoon, I came upon my father in the dining room, sitting at the oval table with his head in his hands, crying. That was the end of my childhood. For I had somehow to absorb the frightening fact that he had drunk too much. He was not the person I knew. The foundations of my world were never again entirely firm.

19 FEBRUARY

Today, Sunday, we went to Westminster Abbey for the morning service as casually as if to a village church. A village is what London feels like. Wherever I look, I see people whom I know either by familiarity with their rosy Anglo-Saxon faces or in history—statues of Nelson, Pitt,

Lord Palmerston. Even Abraham Lincoln, whom I confronted in the park near the Abbey with a special feeling of comradeship: an American on the soil of his forefathers, but grown up out of our prairie, gaunt and raw.

I will leave gladly tomorrow, for here in England I have rounded off my journey by closing the gap between myself at ten and myself fifty-two years later.

Within the full circle of my father's almost eighty years his tears at the Artillery Mansions have a proper place, as all comes to rest in understanding when informed by affection.

I have once again stood in the cloister of Westminster Abbey, as I stood with my mother so many years ago. We had gone there alone together toward the end of our stay in London. My father was "better," but my mother had been changed too by his behavior and it may be that she was moved by her unhappiness to turn away from her private life into the instruction of her daughter. For she changed before my eyes from a sad woman, shoulders drooping under the new British cashmere coat to which she had treated herself, into an incisive and well-informed teacher. We had emerged from the interior of the Abbey into the cloister and my mother explained to me how the great walls had been raised high into the air by way of buttressing. I saw the principle immediately, with the particular vivid pleasure that accompanies an insight in line with one's native bent. I felt as if within my own body the stress of walls against buttresses, buttresses against walls, and by a kind of instant extrapolation how inside and outside match in mutual tension, in people as well as in buildings. I cannot remember that this insight made my father's character clearer to me then, but I do remember feeling that she had opened a way for me by placing in my hand the objective tool of my own intellect. I understood that an idea could become an aspiration, and an aspiration a reality if intelligent and persevering effort were brought to bear.

This memory soars above all that has so widened my perspective on this trip. For it seems to me now that there in Westminster Abbey, at the age of ten, I put my foot on my own way: I would not have to succumb to painful circumstances in life because I could rise above them by using my own resources to turn them to my own purposes.

2 2   F E B R U A R Y

W A S H I N G T O N ,   D . C .

Ever since I left Paris, I have been walking around as if I were balancing on my head a jar of water, anxious lest I spill a single drop of the ever-accumulating impressions Europe was adding to my experience. At home, I can gratefully put down this jar, now brimful. I have had to carry it awkwardly, adjusting my stance under it, because even in the ideal circumstances I enjoyed during my journey, I had to rearrange my habits to accord with those around me.

This morning I woke up at 5:15, about my normal time, so I am on my way out of jet lag, and in my own bed, no more comfortable than the ones I have been sleeping in, but my own. On my bureau, my family photographs are arranged in their accustomed places on freshly ironed embroidered linen; the closets are in order; the mail has been sorted and can wait; my very muscles are happy to be reaching confidently here and there in habitual patterns of work. I am eating oddly—last night a *lot* of asparagus, hot buttered whole-wheat toast, and an apple. I observe that I am dependent on this kind of improvisation and have missed a physical strength I seem to get from choosing and eating what I feel hungry for when I feel hungry; my regimen may make me especially vulnerable to hidden physiological pitfalls I avoid by this kind of apparently impulsive eating. So this morning I can feel myself lining up: east-west-north-south and up-down on my own particular axis of gravity.

Aside from all else, I have learned that I am dependent on affection. I am "the Cat that walks by himself and all places are alike to him" only if I know there is a hearth nearby at which I will be welcome.

My twin sisters were born when I was eighteen months old. Not only were they unusually beguiling babies but also there were two of them, each made even more interesting by contrast to the other in their fraternal twinship. I was shunted aside, naturally enough, but perhaps more harshly than my parents realized as their advent coincided with the departure of my devoted nurse, by whom I had been tenderly introduced into touch with the world, and into trust in it. Fortunately, we had a dog, and it was with him that I was thrust out into our garden "to play." Tawny and brindled, he had lots of energy and kept me what company I had. Little enough though, and I well remember the disconsolate feeling with which I narrowed my expectations, reducing them with a sort of politeness to what my parents were able to provide in the excitement of the household. The politeness assured me of that attention, guaranteed it in effect, as I was being a good girl. My rage at being displaced had to be suppressed. I took to examining grasses and trees and buildings and fences, and to my imagination. The fact of solitude combined with these new interests to form within me a tacit decision to rely on myself, and myself alone. A spot of pain remained: a hot feeling in my chest out of which the fierceness I could not express without the danger of losing all affection added defiance to my independence.

I see this as sad now that I am aging, and in that perspective can observe how I have to an extent deprived myself of a lively emotional exchange within which people can nourish one another from day to day. Just as I substituted for it my self-generated interests in the garden, I later turned my work into a refuge. A fortress, in effect, from which I foray and to which I always return.

The early days of my marriage taught me once again to trust to affection, and once again I was disillusioned, possibly partly by my own hand as I had not formed a sufficiently broad and vital capacity for intimacy. It was not until I separated from James and began to live in the companionship of my children that I came once again to trust. It is this trust that has widened into faith and made the years of my maturity happier than those of my youth.

2 5   F E B R U A R Y

Mary and Charlie are here for a visit. It is a pleasure to reverse roles, to be hostess instead of guest. The company of grown-up children is a unique delight when tastes and interests are in common. Mary and I chat and chat while Charlie, now in the resolute individualism of three and a half, runs around alternately interrupting us and joining in.

Charlie and I have been doing jigsaw puzzles together and it is fun to watch his dexterity. It is fun, too, to hear what he is thinking about now that he is talkative. I feel the same curiosity about him I felt about my children when they were younger, and to an even greater degree still feel: What will they come up with next? This curiosity has been the factor

I have found the most abiding help in my continuing attempt to offset the attachment of motherhood with the objectivity absolutely necessary for peace of mind in the face of the inevitable and inexorable problems that make the lives of my children occasionally difficult and painful.

I have been surprised by how difficult and painful. In a hopeful suspension of logic, I had somehow maintained an expectation that their lives would be smoother than any others I have known. They are not. All I can do is keep them company as they work their way through.

26 FEBRUARY

Europe weaves in and out of my dreams at night and my thoughts during the day. Last night I dreamed of a tangle of dried pomegranate vines with rich round orange fruit dangling among them, and a newly born baby lying in their nest. The round world became golden to me during my weeks abroad. I had not thought that I would find it as interesting as I did. Perhaps I had in my imagination drained it of meaning so I could leave it, when I die, with less grief. In any case, I had conceived of it as a ball of earth, more or less one texture, without surprises in store. Instead, I was over and over brought to a standstill by its beauty and variety, and now, a new baby myself in this respect, I have evolved an opposite point of view: because it is beautiful and varied I can leave it more easily.

Spring

A normal morning after a normal night. I feel balanced and plain.

The paintings I made last summer are framed. They are leaning on wooden horses around the studio, among the sculptures I made at the same time. When the people scheduled to look at them have all done so, I will dispose of them, either to galleries or storage, and pack the studio for transportation to Yaddo, to which I move for nine months as acting executive director on March 28. I look forward with satisfaction to working in Pigeon West. It is a year-round studio, heated. I will need the solid ground of my own work while I do whatever has to be done in a new undertaking.

Last night Sam and I heard the honking of wild geese. "On their way north," said Sam, and in his voice I heard against the background of their calling a note of secure happiness I have not heard from him before. A note that trumpets as clearly as that in the stretched throats of the geese the flight he himself will soon take in his own direction, back to college for his final year.

The sun is shining and it is my sixty-third birthday and I find in myself no trace of any desire to hold him back. Or to hold Alexandra or Mary from their chosen directions. I had first to discover that I *could* not hold them and at the same time retain their respect and spontaneous affection, adjust to that fact, and as peaceably and generously as possible live out the ten or so years it took to thin out the thick bloodstream of placental connection. Our mutual ties are more delicate now. But they are not fragile. The filaments have tensile strength; they can tighten, and I have no doubt they occasionally will, but most of the time they are simply there, not too taut and not too loose.

I have now outlived my mother by almost ten years but she is as vivid to me as she must have been sixty-three years ago this morning, a young woman with her newborn daughter at her side. My father too, in whose attentiveness I always felt myself blossom. I think of them, my sisters and myself, our children and children's children, particularly of my sister Louise's grandchild curled in her daughter's womb. We are ordinary. It is this very ordinariness, the lovely ordinariness all human beings hold in common, that I cherish.

Today I begin to pack my work for Yaddo, myself on the wing.

A burglar came into my studio while I was in Europe. When I first stepped over its threshold on my return, I thought "Someone bad has been in here," but logic said no one had and I scoffed at my imagination. A few days later, I missed some miscellaneous tools I kept in a little basket, mostly Japanese, nothing valuable except to my hand after twenty years of use. I kept thinking the basket would turn up but in packing the studio this afternoon I realized that my two old sanders and a 72-inch steel ruler were also missing.

A new dead-bolt lock now double-bars the studio from the alley. I have bought a new sander—one to replace two but that's the best I can do right now. Theft leaves behind it a meanness that lingers in the atmosphere like a smelly fog. My impression is more of mischief than of evil; an inexperienced sneak thief, I guess, who snatched and ran, for real harm could have been done and was not. What will the thief make out of the transaction? Very little. The Japanese tools were worth scarcely more than nothing: an ingenious blue-handled mat knife; a stout spatula; a painty hammer; a metal opener from the Nippon Paint Company; a well-balanced long knife; two pairs of scissors. I will miss them, and the memories they evoked every time I picked them up.

But a lot is being swept away from me by this move to Saratoga Springs. I shall return in nine months but indeed we cannot step into the same river twice and I and my house and my studio and my belongings will have changed by next January.

My household is packed for my departure to Yaddo tomorrow. I am no longer at home here. In my garden the forsythia is blooming above the frosted grass.

Y A D D O

S A R A T O G A S P R I N G S

N E W Y O R K

A thoughtful drive up here yesterday, almost ten hours of silence. I am in the guest room of the executive director's house. I overlook a lawn of dull grass streaks under snow sloping gradually down toward gleaming nests of twigged bushes bordering stark, bare trees backed by towering dark green pines. An austere scene that matches my grave mood of readiness.

Snow is filling up the woods. Yesterday I walked alone in a wild blizzard.

Curtis Harnack, the executive director of Yaddo, is instructing me in his duties. We quarter the grounds and buildings together. I look and listen carefully.

My daily life could not be more changed. Instead of a solitary effort to maintain a context more or less of my own invention, I find myself becoming a part of a continuity I can serve. I like that very much. More than I would have, had I not realized in Europe the benefactions of community.

There are details to be learned—lots of them—but the principles are becoming clear to me. As far as I can tell now in these very early days, this job primarily demands a discriminating judgment and a state of consciousness that magnetizes all that goes on here without interfering with it.

1 APRIL

Curtis Harnack left today. I feel as if a shawl of well worn material had gently, but inexorably, fallen in clinging folds upon my shoulders.

2 APRIL

My old friend Orion is keeping my company. Every point in his striding constellation glitters with pride of place in the splendor of the country night sky. So Hesiod must have seen him. The stars in the dome circling the horizon intersect the tree stalks that circumscribe the areas of open ground counterpointing the dark reaches among the celestial bodies.

I am lonely. I could not have predicted the precise isolation of leadership.

4 APRIL

Aside from walking, nothing I am doing is automatic. Letters that would usually take me a few minutes to write take time because I have first to find and then to learn new information—as I do almost every minute.

I am living in the executive director's house, which I am rearranging to help myself feel at home. Here in my bedroom, a postcard I bought and framed forty-odd years ago, a Greek marble head of Pallas Athena, hangs opposite my bed above an antique mahogany crib that I have covered with a blue and white flowered cloth on which I have propped up the stuffed animals my grandchildren sleep with when they visit me. They are comforting to me too. On a round table by double glass doors facing south, a ranunculus of purest yellow coils petal on petal like a medieval rose. A birthday present from Sam; he picked it up from the greenhouse on the Washington Cathedral close while on a morning run so it links that familiar place to this. On a woven cane rocker, my two Indian shawls, gray and brown. My bureau is immense, lots of drawers of convenient sizes. On it, next to a filigreed Tiffany lamp, a triptych of Lake George —green mountains and woods, blue water and sky— painted on glass framed in gilt; the center panel must have been broken and has been replaced by a mirror. That is typical of Yaddo; when anything here breaks, it is, if possible, frugally mended. By my bed, within easy reach of my hand, a telephone, a flashlight, and a list of numbers for emergency.

The dimensions of my job are beginning to emerge as if fog were lifting unevenly over an unknown landscape. I more and more understand that I have undertaken an incalculable responsibility.

Early tomorrow morning I go by train to New York City for a Yaddo benefit that night, and a meeting of the National Council for Yaddo the next day, returning late in the evening.

5   APRIL

Administration is essentially a matter of linked causation: a task is not undertaken for its own sake but for a purpose to which it is causal. I am going to spend today and tomorrow in activity aimed toward raising money for Yaddo so that artists can work here and the world can learn from what they make. This is an honorable cause that cleaves close to the line of my lifetime endeavor. But the fact remains that I will be doing what I would never do naturally and that in itself can be a little harmful in the short run and very harmful in the long because unnatural behavior tends to harden sensitivity. Potentially hazardous, too, because it is easy to slip into rationalizations, mistaking means for ends, and then to become attached to them, to ancillary "success."

I have enunciated these ideas to look at them so that I can see the principles involved, implied. And to remind myself that a detached, objective frame of mind is necessary for right action.

7 APRIL

I returned from New York City last night. When I descended from the train in Albany and saw the member of the staff who had come to meet me, I quietly resumed what is becoming the habit of my new role. I asked questions, he answered, and I gently picked up these threads of information as if they were reins.

While I was in New York, I had time to think over my position at Yaddo. The departure of Curtis Harnack, for whom the staff have affection as well as respect, has sent shock waves through their community. I spent last week meeting these waves and trying to lull them. I wish to become taken for granted as rapidly as feasible. But the board of directors has reposed their trust in me and I must do this job in my own way. As an interim executive director —and I am at pains to make it clear to the staff that I am a seneschal for Curtis Harnack, who returns on 1 January 1985—I do not aim to make any substantive changes. Just in the difference of our natures, however, I will be working from a point of view tangential to his, and this must be clarified if I am to adjust to them and they to me.

The two days in New York were a strain. I find myself receiving there also the kind of guarded, watchful attention I have been surprised by here at Yaddo. I am used to moving around unnoticed—impossible in a position of authority. I depend on slipping in and slipping out of situations. I cannot do so here, but it is probably useful that I am accustomed to trying not to make heavy weather of my dealings in the world.

11 APRIL

Nadir this morning. I came stark awake at four and watched the first light develop the trees against the sky and the grass against the banks of receding snow. I am thankful that my sister Louise is visiting me, an affectionate, familiar presence, and I am thankful for the sovereign beauty of Yaddo, which I am slowly realizing is a powerful source of strength.

I have not had a job as unremitting as this since I was in my twenties; I teach at the university only two days a week. It seems to me that I no sooner leave the office than I am returning to it, and I often have dinner with the guests—a pleasure as I enjoy their interesting company, but one almost fatally tempered by my official position. Also, I am accustomed to solving problems by myself. Here they necessarily involve other people who have longer experience with the particularities than I and on whose information I have to rely, to pick my way through as through a thicket. Because I have never before been in a position of formal leadership, I have never had to adjust under so much pressure and so rapidly to so many inexorably moving events. An institution keeps on running day and night. I am forced not only to keep pace but also to try to run a little ahead so that I can make decisions with a leeway of time in which to think.

The strain is letting up a little. Partly because I am becoming accustomed to my duties and partly because I am changing the way I hold Yaddo in my consciousness. I continue to feel, from my observation of Curtis Harnack as well as now from my own experience, that the fortitude of the director is in subtle ways critical to Yaddo's protection of the artists who are guests here. Not that this at all implies interference with them. Rather a running of interference *for* them, forethought in order that they may in no way be disturbed in their work. I like doing this. Having enjoyed the unique ease bestowed by such care here, I am happy to be able to help to give it to others. I had thought before I undertook it that this responsibility would involve a particular kind of conscious attention and I was right about that, but I am finding that this attention is comparable to the way in which I have always held my households in my mind—carefully, but without undue concern.

This is not entirely a surprise, but I *am* surprised by the degree to which I am beginning to depend on the turn of season here, on the subtle seduction of living in the country. A seduction that I can fully enjoy because I can count on the continuity of a long period of time here. I feel myself sensuously, even languorously, falling under the spell of nature. I watch the buds swell. The line snow draws on the rippling lakes changes every day. The other night I heard a crash outside the door of my house and, when I opened it, saw a fox streaking away from the woodshed. About five feet from nose to tip of tail, with dark copper-red fur, lustrous and fluffed out all over as if vibrating; wild and remote in wildness, authoritative paw on earth. A pungent smell lingered in the air.

20 APRIL

Ever since years ago when I read C. S. Forester's novels on the life of Horatio Hornblower in the British navy, I have pondered on what it would be like to be the captain of a ship. That kind of independence of character became one of the standards I applied to people, and it was a facet of my decision to take this job that in a very modest way I would be testing myself. Horatio Hornblower asked Mr. Bush, his second-in-command, only technical questions; he never told him his tactical plans until it became necessary; he acted only when he chose to, and then acted decisively. I am finding this habit wise. Every natural impulse toward dependence weakens me. I can seek advice, but I cannot ask for help.

24 APRIL

I have always dreaded being snared. I am. I entered this situation of my own free will, for purposes that do not fail me, but the fact remains: I am netted.

Tonight I will have dinner with the guests: their working lives true me. My own working life cannot because I have none, or so little that it serves only to fret the edges of my mind, to place me in conflict. For the first time since my work steadied under me in 1961, I am having intractable difficulty shifting gears from the kind of energy I use in regular life to the utterly different kind I use in my studio. I think this is because I am being forced to deal with an unaccustomed number of unfamiliar variables, one of which is the immediate pressure of other people's personalities. I am used to working alone except at the university, and the drive there and back isolates that area of my life. Most of the Yaddo work necessarily involves interaction. And an overwhelming number of pieces of paper: a linear progression of constantly changing flat thin things in my hands; I miss the solidity of work in art and the depth of concentration. These pieces of paper most often require only a second or so of attention—I read, decide, and pass on to the next. Shutter-flashes of information without intrinsic interest, but necessary to the understanding of Yaddo that I must form in order to sustain its momentum in a proper direction. I am used to moving easily from one familiar area to another— home to studio to children to friends to university to dealer to museum, and so on, touching down lightly. Here the work I have undertaken is so amorphous and unfamiliar that I cannot even discern its parameters.

Last evening I saw two deer. They live somewhere in the sandy pine-barren woods surrounding my house to the south. I did not know the deer were there until I saw them prancing in a twilit field. Just so, I discover new facts every day, and each one changes my perspective on the tensile field of force that is Yaddo.

The furnace in the Mansion has been turned on for the first wave of summer guests, who will arrive in two weeks. The ladies have begun cleaning. I went to see how it was going yesterday afternoon. The housekeeper and I had a fine time deciding on rug cleaning and lamp fixtures and where best to place furniture. Blessedly familiar: a house to keep.

The Mansion is the principal dwelling at Yaddo. It was designed in 1893 by William Halsey Wood to replace the original house that burned down in 1891. He patterned it on Haddon Hall, built in Derbyshire in the fifteenth century, but Spencer and Katrina Trask gave him a great deal of advice so that the Mansion innocently combines eclectic architectural elements in a way more idiosyncratic than historical. It is for this reason, despite its imposing siting and size and its gray stones, endearing. It is closed in the winter to save the cost of heating it, so for eight months of the year Yaddo can accommodate only twelve guests, who have their meals in the Yaddo library on the second floor of the original servants' quarters and carriage house. When the winter houses are supplemented by the Mansion, Yaddo expands to take twenty-six guests. It is this expansion that is about to take place. I am glad that I have had time to become accustomed to the routine here. The executive director has two assistants during the summer, artists who live and work as the guests do but settle new guests in their quarters and generally help out. They act to tether the community: fixed points of reference for the artists who come and go.

25 APRIL

Here in this deliberate northern spring I am day by day convinced by the evidence of my eyes that the earth is alive. Where except from within the teleology of its own substance could the changes I observe arise? If I reverse the film of what I have seen around me for the last four weeks, I watch a greening melt away into brown earth slashed with snowbanks, into blizzard white. If I run it forward again, the blizzard thins; the snow gradually shrinks into streaks, and vanishes; the earth brightens visibly greener every single day and stalked trees slowly mist with a bitter yellow now evolving toward bluish green in tiny butterflies of leaves. Violets drift along the folds of land. It is as if I were watching a pale face slowly blush, and am becoming friendly with the personality behind its expression.

2 8 APRIL

Just as I yearned to converse with Henry James in Paris, I yearn to talk over all this nature with D. H. Lawrence. My own edges are somehow blurring into union with it. Yesterday I knelt over the flower beds around my house, pulling out dry stalks, clearing from the pungent earth at their feet stout, poignant shoots. I do not know what of. Here even the familiarity of gardening is a little guarded. I did not plant these plants. I will take care of them through only one season. I cannot plan projections of what the beds will look like in a few years, one (if not the chief) pleasure of an inexperienced, romantic gardener like me. This ground is no more mine than the house I live in. The desk I use in the office is not my own. The studio in which I hope to be able to work if I can clear my way as I cleared that of the plants is not my own. I am homesick. Nothing here is wholly familiar to me.

I have watched for the bloat of ego that being acting executive director might blow me up with. The opposite is happening. Because I am isolated while I am here, as if I were in the controlled environment of a precisely timed scientific experiment, I am seeing with almost terrifying clarity how utterly transient I am, essentially irrelevant to Yaddo save to serve day by day. Night by night, I look at the stars when the sky is clear and draw beneath them a line around the ground I am supposed to guard. When I arrived,

I tried to spread out my consciousness to fill this circumference, as if to lock it magically into safety. I thought that was what guardianship was—a watchful attentiveness that is a particular kind of love. As the days have stretched into weeks, and I have looked in the crannies of all the buildings and walked the woods in different weathers, I have realized that that is out of proportion. The wild fox told me in the flash of his wild presence. He walked the ground as if he were its and it were his, unparticularized. And since I saw him I have been more fox than acting executive director. D. H. Lawrence would understand that better than I do.

I am now so far from bloat that it's all I can do to keep myself together. The sun interpenetrates the earth; they have business with each other. Air and I are somewhere in between.

This tentative new area of feeling is similar to that at the beginning of a friendship. I am being forced by the experiences I am having with the natural world around me to recognize that I am living in touch with another living being —I do not know what other word to use, so quick and near do I feel this presence.

It is as if this period at Yaddo is a microcosm of a human life stripped of some of the possibilities of illusion. I am here for a specific length of time. I cannot subside into the relaxed state of mind that the possibility of open-ended continuity evokes. That is what home is—the implicit promise of stable continuation. It is as if I were being forced to recognize what human life actually is: a delineated period of time during which one abides without the possibility of continuity. It is as if life itself were, like Yaddo, an institution. I am realizing this with a force I have never hitherto experienced except now and then in what I thought of as moments of enlightenment, with emphasis on the "moments"—the fact that they broke the usual reality of my situation. Now I am feeling this balance very gradually reversing. I am beginning to live as if I were continuously *not* here and only in moments here, because I can count the moments, the hours, the days, the months that constitute my term here. No denial of this transitory state is possible and, by extension, I am less able to delude myself that my life on earth is in this sense different in any way. I live on earth as I live at Yaddo: for a period during which I take care of what happens to me as best I can.

Jonquils, my favorite flowers, are blowing here and there all over Yaddo.

Last night after dinner with the guests I typed up the final papers for a trip to New York City tomorrow—two days of meetings. The sheets lie in seven neat piles in my studio on the table I had hoped, and still hope, to draw on. One last conference this morning; two telephone appointments at eight and eight-thirty tonight. Otherwise, I am taking some time today to do what I now think of as a rest: something customary that doesn't have officially to be put on paper, or delayed, or relayed succinctly, tactfully, or sequentially to someone else.

The laundromat: I sit with assorted folk idly flipping a tattered magazine while the machines spin and the cars cruise on the road outside; ironing—wonderful to have *things* under my hands again; reading: *Diana of the Crossways* —I am interested in George Meredith's deep loyalty to women and his subtle understanding of physical passion; and lying in the spring sun. Ordinariness.

At the board of directors' meeting in New York, I sat for the first time at the executive end of the immense, immaculately white-clothed oval table on the fourth floor of the Century Association. The view from there is different. Our deliberations were tangential to the directors' lives, central to mine.

Self-definition is a little lame. Because in two days of meetings I was treated as acting executive director, I am reenforced in that role. Being treated as an artist in 1962 had the same effect on me at first; I had to give credence to a definition of myself not altogether my own. And when I was appointed professor at the University of Maryland, I noticed that even though nothing else had changed, the title of Professor conferred on me weight, as if my skeleton had become slightly but perceptibly denser.

Yesterday I began to work on my sculpture. I am, I hope, learning how to shift from Yaddo's business to the studio and to my personal life. I seem to be adjusting to Yaddo as if I were at home here, accepting it as continuity even though I know that it is not.

The land from which I watched the snows recede is exuberant with tender bright green grass. Jonquils and forsythia have bloomed and faded; scarlet tulips and blue and white hyacinths cluster about my house, purple pansies border my lawn. The birds are building nests the same way I am learning to do my job here, by faithfully collecting and weaving bits and pieces.

There should be a word to substitute for "children" when they have grown up. But that would perhaps lead to new words for "mother" and "father," and to a loss of the historical continuity that is the heart of a family.

Alexandra is now twenty-eight, Mary twenty-six, and Sam twenty-three. Their adult lives weave in and out of mine, embroidered by the lives of my grandsons. I am living long enough to see the pattern of four generations. I made decisions for my children based in large part on the pattern of my parents. Now I see those my daughters make for their children, sometimes in line with mine and sometimes so different that they introduce threads entirely new. I was more open about my feelings than my parents had been; my children talk even more openly to their children. They ask their children more questions about how they in turn feel. By the same token, they ask me for explanations of my behavior to them when they were little. I am led to reexamine this behavior with them and in the course of exchanging our points of view we continually bring all our lives up-to-date.

When Alexandra was a few months old, her pediatrician noticed that she had an extra roll of fat on one leg, an indication that she might have been born with one leg longer than the other. I took her to be X-rayed, and then had to wait three days for the medical verdict. I had by that time realized that I was not the perfect mother I had hoped to be, and had concluded sturdily that Alexandra would have to adjust to me, to my character, as I was finding that I had to adjust to hers. While I waited to hear whether she had a birth defect, I added to this decision another: she would have to adjust to her life herself. I would help her to do so courageously with every ounce of my strength, but the balance of adjustment would have to be on her side: the pain of operations, the acceptance of affliction. It turned out that her legs were fine, but it was that experience that set up in me a certain expectation in my children of independent hardihood. Within this context, I perhaps came to take their autonomy too much for granted, and in doing so may not have been as sensitive to their feelings as I ideally would like to have been. But the fact remains that a healthy adjustment between parents and children is mutual and has to go both ways.

This point of view strengthens me while I watch my daughters bringing up their children. It also reenforces my fortitude as I come to realize my shortcomings during their childhood. I am as motivated to clarify our history together as they are; their futures are as dear to me as they are to themselves. And my own future is also important to me. I do not wish to come to death without having understood my life in as wide and deep a scope as possible.

This involves thinking of our lives together in the largest context possible, and for me that seems to be the operation of the law of karma: the law that for every psychological action there is a meet reaction. These actions and reactions are conceived of as extending from one lifetime to another, a series of lifetimes constituting the history of a soul's evolution toward perfection. I do not *believe* in this formulation. I simply hold it in hypothesis, and operate within it because it is the most intelligent and comprehensive context that my life has presented to me.

My principal reaction to the newly evolving relationships between my children and me is not an undue dwelling on my effect upon them but gratitude that I am alive to join them in a mutual effort to understand ourselves. I am even more grateful for them than for myself, as my parents' deaths deprived me of what they could have contributed to our mutual comprehension. I have had to come alone, without the correction of their view, to the tender perspective of understanding. This perspective is a form of liberation from the past that I am very glad I can help my children provide for themselves.

Summer

I am making frequent trips to New York City on Yaddo affairs, most of them involving the ritual of formal, professional meetings. Last Tuesday I went to a series of such meetings in Wall Street. I was early and had time to walk along the strait canyons between the towering buildings that slice the sky as they do in Piero della Francesca's Sansepolcro, but way up so high that there is no feeling of human scale. I have never before been in a space so extremely narrow, strict, overwhelming, and intellectual. I was giddy. In my blue linen skirt and white cotton blouse, I felt like a plant in a rock tumbler.

This feeling I carried with me into the boardrooms where we met. I wondered how people adjusted to such an environment day after day and in looking around with this in mind I came to notice how we acted.

We tend to mix genders when we arrange ourselves around a table for meetings. A sort of accommodation is made by the men for the women: they make space for us. They are ever-so-slightly polite, we are ever-so-slightly grateful. When we stand up at the end of a meeting, we all give ourselves a metaphorical shake that is only partly the relief of having concluded our business: we are all released from the effort of fitting ourselves together.

When men speak in these meetings, women relax; when women speak, men grow tense. I have the impression that they never know what a woman is going to say, whereas they are reasonably sure what a man will address himself to and how he will do it. So are the women; for them, too, men tend to be predictable. Women listen to women with a different kind of attention, and part of it may be loyalty to our gender: we want all of us to do well, as if we have the esprit de corps of subalterns among generals.

7   J U N E

I have been thinking about the crystals I saw at Crystal Resources in New York last week and wondering why they affected me so strongly. Masses of naked rock as large as four feet across, split in such a way that they were revealed to be hollow like opened melons: shallow caves bristling with sparkling, varicolored translucent spikes. Rimmed by coarsely pitted, brownish-grayish stone and filled with solidified light, they were revelations of how the insides of things cannot always be imagined from their appearance. Of the surprises the divine can spring on the human.

They were beautiful. First by way of this metaphor. Second in form, as the shapes in their interiors varied from crystals a foot or so in length and thick as swords to tiny glistening facets. Third in color: palest amethysts to deepest purples, yellows buttercup to saffron, impenetrable blacks hinting in their depths the darknesses of dreams, and whites that took my breath away, promises of an unimaginable perfection just beyond their catching. They were beautiful, but their beauty was ancillary to their meaning. When I put a hand carefully into their hollows, not touching, it tingled as if in some palpably effervescent water, and I felt curiously exhilarated.

The crystals seem to embody time, to render its mysterious operation visible. I feel a kind of joy in their presence. I have no more access to a cognitive understanding of the laws in accordance with which earth was over millennia pressed into these strange and splendid shapes than I do of the laws I intuit as determining the turns of a course of events. I simply feel as if the crystals put me briefly in touch with truth. In their light, I seem to know with certainty that this life I am living with such absorption is also an exemplification of some kind. As if I were, in this body, an example of a self I do not know and that I may be in the process of developing, or of discovering.

8 JUNE

Woods now wall my house in dappled greens striated by the pinky-tan boles of taller trees silhouetted against the sky I watch change. Deer come to the edge of my lawn. Their coats are sleek and their sides bulge with the new plenty of early summer. Foxes come too. The vixen is bolder than the fox; she trots across the lawn quite openly, looking neither to the right nor to the left, casually. Her fur is not as spectacular as his but has the appeal of motley: russets and ochers and blackish grays. I don't feel like anthropomorphizing these animals I am living with but it did cross my mind as

I watched her the other day that that vixen would have a tale to tell over a cup of tea.

We are now at full capacity. The guests are working steadily. Their faces show the strain. The other night at dinner a man who had lived in Japan as a child suggested that Yaddo is like the sites of Shinto shrines: a place charged with divine force. I instantly took his point. Some atmosphere facilitates work here. This is partly due to the almost palpable energy generated by a number of artists hard at work, but also to something in the air at Yaddo. I always feel it when I enter between the granite gates and wind into the grounds over the causeway dividing two of the lakes: a curious heightening of perception.

20 JUNE

Living in an aging body is an odd business, and business it is, as it has to be paid attention to. My turn toward aging began when I was fifty-nine and confounded me for almost three years. It seemed as if one day I was as strong as I had been all my adult life and the next found myself stuck in a balky vehicle. My endurance fluctuated and every time it did so decreased, as if I were descending a mountain along a path of successive gradations sinking toward I knew not where. I was scared, and flailed around as if to stir up a wind that would push me back up. I constantly overdid because I had no way of gauging how much energy I could count on and kept forgetting how I was changing. I was in the position of a spendthrift who had regularly to retire to debtors' prison, alternately overactive for my capacity and exhausted. These abrupt sine curves threatened my psychological security as I began to doubt my ability to handle my life intelligently.

More and more often I had to give in to prudence, essentially a matter of accepting diminishment as severe as if my bones were thinning inside my flesh, becoming lighter, more brittle, less reliable. And since I always think of my skeleton as a sculptural armature, I had trouble resisting an image of myself as subsiding without its support into a formless pile of clay. Very gradually, I began to realize that my reservoir of physical strength was silently and mysteriously drying up. It was during this period that I drove over icy roads to the Cumberland Gap in the darkening winter evening to pick up Sam. That experience of panic marked the end of my flailing. Routed, I began to examine my whole state more objectively, and reluctantly but realistically to submit to new limitations. After months and months of experimentation, I leveled off a little after my sixty-second birthday. Prudence has become a habit.

I still do not like the diminishment. I can't imagine that anyone would. My imagination is unaffected. I plainly see an entire course of action lying ahead of me, and then have to come to a full stop, invent for it an economic program based on revised predicates of energy, and proceed deliberately. Essentially, I have been through a kind of second adolescence, one of involution rather than evolution: the end, death, instead of a life to be lived.

There are compensations. A slower pace reveals to me details apparent only to someone who is taking time to notice them and paradoxically also gives me a distanced perspective on events, since I have to restrain myself from dashing in to engage in them hot and heavy. It is as if I were tuning in to a deeper, slower resonance in music I have been listening to all my life without realizing that this profundity underlay more lively tunes.

I am even beginning to appreciate some of these changes

that age has initiated. A whole day of rest, for example, would have been unthinkable (literally—I would not have thought of it) a few years ago. Now I almost, not quite, take it for granted that once in a while I have to cut a day entirely out of my pattern of work and just leave that hole in my life. I have begun to enjoy what I put into this interim: reading, writing leisurely letters for pleasure, gardening, washing and ironing clothes, sewing, knitting; sometimes just lying in the sun. These cut-out days may be adumbrations of what old age is like if it is privileged by way of health and a reasonable amount of money. I have sometimes wondered how it would feel to get up in the morning and do what I wanted, as I used to on the Saturdays of my school days.

22 JUNE

Yesterday afternoon when I woke up from a nap after a morning of work on my sculptures, the thought stepped quietly into my tired mind that I could simply stop making the effort to translate myself into visibility in art. I carefully examined this proposition. An end to encrusted, painty clothes and the wear and tear of ascending and descending ladders; an end to crouching on the floor to see color from a different angle in a different light; an end to catching and tediously fixing tiny fissures in the striation of wood; an end to the demands that handling finished work in the world make on my equilibrium. But this last clause snagged and I suddenly realized that I had been hurt by my exclusion from the survey of contemporary painting and sculpture mounted by the Museum of Modern Art to mark the opening of its recent renovation. The museum owns *Catawba,* a 1962 sculpture. I had to conclude as I walked through the galleries last week that my work had been judged not important enough for inclusion. While I was there I took this fact in stride, struck as I was by a splendid plenitude of the fine work of my generation of American artists. At the time I felt only a generous joy that I have been privileged to live in this era of art, to see and to understand with a delight that had nothing to do with my own work how much beauty and truth had been brought into the world in this country during the last forty years. But a barb apparently remains, slender as the thorn of a wild rose.

I continue to consider stopping work. I could cut the Gordian knot, give my work to my children and retreat into the jobs that put food in my mouth and underwrite the financial security of my family, now including another generation. That would perhaps be a sensible plan. Honest enough too.

But not courageous.

Like all crucial decisions, this one has already been made by the history of my life. My sculptures live in my mind. I can rebuff them only at some psychic peril too deep for articulation.

Also, I have a sturdy loyalty to my work that owes nothing to any opinion any other person might have of it. I have faith in it, virtual trust.

Piero della Francesca apparently lost interest in painting toward the end of his life and took to strict mathematical analyses of the laws of perspective. If I find that I too lose interest in my work, I will stop making it. But that would be a decision intrinsic to the context of my life, inevitable.

28 JUNE

Summer is thick now. The spring fawns have been born; the vixen has lately been invisible. The groundhog who lives near my house waddles about complacently, either fat or pregnant, an endearing shape. The Yaddo rose garden is in glorious bloom. I am thinking of buying new carp for the fountain to replace those that died last winter in the spring-fed pond to which they are moved every autumn. Three weak trees have been cut down; one of these had been leaning over a building and now that danger is eliminated. But there are limitless potentialities for disaster in a place this size. Even bolstered by matching limitless financial resources, we would have to cope with one after another. This is no job for a faint heart.

Mine is not faint but I am feeling worn. There is something insidious about this enveloping a responsibility, and if I am not careful in the way I think about it I could begin to feel as if its pressure were so close that the very air were evaporating around me.

1 0   J U L Y

Twice in the course of Yaddo work yesterday I noticed in the eyes of the staff a natural turning toward me for executive decision. An equally natural response met this turn. We all now take me for granted.

The large sculpture I am working on is at once strange to me because I do not know its heart, except as a tremble in my own, and familiar because it looks to me like mine. As I work on it, I scarcely dare breathe lest the tension between me and it will break.

This state of mind is familiar to me. Although it is a strain, I am used to it and feel comfortable with it. When I am working this way, I feel balanced, poised on a straight line that runs from deep down in the ground under my feet up to where I do not know.

When last week in Cambridge, Massachusetts, I turned south toward the Charles River and raked my eye over the red brick, white-clapboard-turreted Harvard Houses, my heart grew heavy beneath my ribs. I crossed the river against my own reluctance and drove along Memorial Drive toward Eliot House in the whispering clangor of dead men.

Stephen Brooks, innocently profligate, who cheerfully used to call himself "cash-another-check-Brooks." Lanky, with one of those hewn heads that with age grizzle gracefully into distinction, but age was what he wasn't to have, and he died in the sand of Africa. My cousin, Arthur Derby, the first Harvard student I ever knew, so classical a golden youth that he defined Greece for me. His bones rock in the Sea of Japan. And others, whom I knew and did not know, who passed through Harvard on their way to peril and, often, to death. How did they do it? I still ask myself. How leave their lives in the glorious promise of their early manhood, without any of the mitigation of the disappointed hopes and sustained efforts with which maturity can wear down a heart? I see their eyes and when I look into them I see that they are wry. They look back at me as if from a distance, and seem ruefully to ask: What is to be expected from life but expendability? A fair question, but one it has taken me a slow lifetime to come to. James's death—for I first met him in Cambridge, in a naval uniform, just returned from kamikaze battles, the gilt on his cap tarnished by the salt of the Pacific—returns to my mind. Surely people can accept death because they know in some ordinarily inaccessible part of themselves that every *single* life is expendable within the wider context of a series of successive lives, each articulated under the aegis of eternity.

Harvard Square, a village crossroads in the 1940s when I lived in Cambridge, is now a cluttered intersection jammed with so many different kinds of people that the students no longer dominate the scene, scarcely even dot it. I could have been in Milwaukee. My twin sisters, whom I had driven to see, have measured this change in their Cantabridgian lives, as we have measured others of which we spoke during my visit, sometimes with sadness, sometimes with laughter. We have reached our sixties. Our differences in temperament remain, along with the sisterhood within which we try now, toward the end of our lives, to make an alignment toward our inevitable deaths.

The adjustments of age are more difficult than those of youth. Our psychic systems creak like old, worn engines, ratchetted unpredictably by the rust of attachment to our own ways. We have to force ourselves to face up to facts we might prefer to elide, and to abnegate where we might prefer to dominate. We can no longer afford the expression of all the privileges of individuality if we are to enjoy the kindliness of family understanding. I am now the only person alive who remembers my sisters in their cradles. They preserve me in comparable ways. Louise's memory of my back as I walked toward school recalled me to the line of my independence, and fortified me. We are irreplaceable to one another.

And equally so to the generations below us. After Cambridge, I drove to Westchester County where Alexandra is established for the summer. Sammy is now six, Alastair four. Brown and mosquito-bitten, they are merry to find themselves for the first time living in the country. Sammy has his mother's interest in little living things—Alexandra at three had what her father called "a slug farm" by the kitchen door of our house in Belvedere, California. Sammy's interest is more abstract. He watches more than he touches. He has my mother's fastidiousness, and something of her remote quality too; his eyes hide more than they reveal. He depends on his younger brother, and rightly so as Alastair is very, very steady. The sun in his sky is his affection for his family. He has no idea how vulnerable that makes him. We all watch him with the special tenderness with which we would guard him throughout his life—if we could. They play all day long and drop off to sleep in the gloaming with delicious ease, smelling faintly of grass and the copper little boys somehow secrete when they are active and happy.

Alexandra is "finished" now, grown up. She commutes to New York for her job in an art gallery where she works to support her family, but she could do that and not be grown up. Her adulthood is written in her mien. She moves as if pivoted on the point of a personal gyroscope she trusts and does not intend to have fooled with. I was glad to observe this, and respect it, but I felt a slight sadness too. I trace her back to the moment of her birth and forward in her sons: a trajectory along which I know her, and hold her in my heart.

24 JULY

The paradoxical promise of sexual love—self-expression and self-forgetting—can haunt older people, for imagination does not age.

Some years ago, my eye fell on a letter written to Ann Landers by a woman made eloquent by her experience with sexuality in late middle life. Widowed, she met and married a man with a remarkable capacity for intimacy. His habit was to return at about five-thirty from a day's rough labor and eat a hearty supper. After a short rest, he shaved, had a hot shower, and put on clean pajamas. Freshened, he enjoyed going immediately to bed with her. He taught her to lie in his arms while they leisurely talked over their lives—what they had done and how they had felt at the time, their assessment of their experience. In the course of this interesting exchange, both of them clean and warm and comfortable, she remarked with simple sweetness that they often turned to one another, their compatibility gradually deepening toward sexual union.

Recently the memory of this letter collided with an examination of a series of drawings that Picasso made in his seventies. He repeatedly juxtaposes a young and voluptuous woman with an artist-figure mercilessly depicted as the clown of his youthful paintings satirized into ugly, silly age. These figures act out a masque of sexuality, interchangeable male and female roles delineated by facial masks they hold up to one another. The ecstatic mutuality informing sexual interchange is at once mocked and, in a way most profoundly touching, celebrated.

I am reminded of Michelangelo's regret in his old age that he had not devoted himself to God instead of to art. He had spent his life by that time in an attempt to mediate by way of beauty the relationship between humankind and the divine. It was too late for him to redirect his effort, as Picasso implies that it is too late for him to experience the rich eloquence of sexual union. Both appear to have come toward the end of their lives to a recognition that the most valuable of all human potentialities is some form of shared subjectivity by way of which individuality is at once most fully actualized, and transcended.

I have been thinking about this yearning for union as I age because I am finding that it is an urge so fundamental to me that it is not fading. For the first years of my life, I looked around to see what matched me so that I could express this desire to find enhancement of my identity within a context that would give me both confirmation and expansion. The people around me, except for my baby nurse, who left about the time of my sisters' birth and died soon after, and my father when he was well, were not only inexpressive but preoccupied. I turned to my physical environment, to the garden's trees, grass, flowers, bushes. The garden was bisected by a brick path. I noticed the pattern of its rectangles, and then saw that they were repeated in the brick walls of the houses of Easton; their verticals and horizontals were also to be found in clapboard walls, in fences, and in lattices. In my passion (no other word will do for the ardor I felt) for something to love, I came to love these proportions—and years later, in 1961 when I was forty years old, this love welled up in me and united with my training in sculpture to initiate and propel the work that ha⁻ occupied me ever since.

When in my early adolescence I learned from the classical novels my mother read me that men and women felt ardor for one another, I transferred part of my hope for enhancement to the expectation implicit in this fact. Later my mother explained the process of sexual love to me. Such intimacy seemed to my naive mind to hold infinite promise. During the years of my growing maturity, and in my maturity, this compound of emotional and physical union so preoccupied me as to form the major affective segment of the circumference and horizon of my hope. Very gradually I came to understand the range of potentiality within the union of man and woman, and even more gradually to recognize that this potentiality was not only finite but also subject to the unpredictable hazards of misunderstanding, of crisscrossed motivations. I actually arrived at this understanding in 1961, and it now seems to me that the mechanism by way of which I then turned my major force from my private emotional life to my work was the same as that by which I turned from people to proportions.

Now that I am in my sixties, I find myself on the brink of another turn. I have fairly thoroughly explored the union of my feeling with what my hand can make. Not entirely. I will not, as far as I can tell, give up that pursuit. But I begin to envision a union beyond it, and this one *does* seem to offer infinite potentiality: a yearning toward the divine which I intuitively experience as immanent in all that I have known and know. I will in time come to this interesting union by way of death.

2 6 J U L Y

I think that the Yaddo staff has come to trust me because of a particular kind of truthfulness. When I have been mistaken, I have been ready to say so, and have found ready understanding. A mutual recognition of common fallibility has been a key. I feel reasonably certain that every single member of this staff has accurately observed my strengths and weaknesses as an administrator and has come to depend on my strengths and, in a friendly way, to take up the slack of my weaknesses.

Another key is the detachment I have myself worked hard to maintain. The staff picks up the fact that I am serving Yaddo just as they are, so the peaceableness we try to make here for the artists is an achievement of which we can all claim equal part.

Sam has been spending the summer here, living in the writer's studio on the lawn of my house. He has been working at a printing press on tiring odd-hour shifts and came home the other day with a virus. Late yesterday evening I was lying on the couch alternately watching the languid locust trees against the sky and reading *The Saratogian,* a delightful newspaper that tells me who has been arrested, who married, who died, plus just enough for the uses of daily life about the world's affairs, when he called me. Something strangled in his voice brought me to my feet. His temperature was 103.4°. The doctor. Into a tepid bath. Medicine and alcohol rub. Fresh pajamas. Fresh bed. Cracked ice to suck. His temperature dropped to 102°. And as twilight deepened into night, gradually continued to drop. I felt his hand cooling in mine as we talked peacefully of this and that.

A Christmas, the happiest he remembered, that we had all spent in the Virginia household of beloved friends who relished as we did conversation and snowy walks and charades after dinner and music sung in random voices around the piano. My generation of these friends has died but their children and my children water their memory. Even little Charlie remembers "Aunt Syddy" and it was the patchwork unicorn she gave him that he brought here with him two weeks ago. We talked of Sam's generation, of his friends who are over the years becoming to him what mine were to me while they lived; of their passage out of boyhood, here equitable, there explosive. As we talked, I felt the fear evoked by his illness evaporate into the normal history we were retelling one another. One future day we would say, "Do you remember . . . ?" and recall all this.

The insights of fever can be revelatory. I am now sick with Sam's virus. I just saw from my bed the first sign of autumn: a slender oval yellow leaf that slowly fell aslant my window. This illness has taken me by surprise in the sharp shape of fear. I feel the cold blade of mortality. I am going to die. Sam, who is now reading here in my room as I write, is going to die. Alexandra and Mary, Sammy, Charlie and Alastair are going to die. My sisters are going to die. One by one we will fall, as casually and as soon forgotton as that first autumn leaf. No word on page, no color set free in space, no act or thought or feeling or hard-wrung conceptualization will matter a whit.

The office work is very demanding these days. No letup at all. The turn toward the winter solstice is shortening the hours of light. The trees are here and there spattered with scarlet. I am virtually never alone. In my circumstances, the gifts of Yaddo tantalize. I cannot help regarding the visiting artists with a little envy.

Last night I awoke from a bad dream. My goddaughter and I were shopping in an exotic store when someone dashed up to me and said that Mary and Charlie had been hurt. "Badly?" I asked. "Yes, her shoulder."

We hurried out into a deserted two-way esplanade of grass-grown cement punctuated by derelict telephone poles. Dusty, gray-green bushes straggled about. After rushing some distance, we saw Mary crouched on the median strip over Charlie. When she lifted her head, she rose and came toward me, crying, and I saw that her face was pale as milk; her crooked left shoulder and dangling arm, bared by a torn black cotton blouse, were blue with bruises. Behind her, Charlie's little face was as pale, his mouth open in shock and in his eyes an expression of betrayal as if he were thinking, "Why did they deceive me by making me think I was safe when this was true all the time?" My goddaughter, who is Charlie's godmother, rushed to him with one of her lovely soft cries and gathered him into her arms. I held Mary while she sobbed and told me how it got dim and they hadn't been able to see and had stumbled over something, she didn't know what. All the while, the sky hung low over us all, a no-color color, utterly expressionless.

As I came slowly to my senses, I echoed Mary's heartbreak. The essence of what she was telling me was that she had been as careful as she could and that all her care had been of no avail: she could not protect herself and her son. Indeed the truth, I was able to think as I changed my position in bed to break the circuit of my panic. Charlie was right. We live in a deception we acknowledge in mutual reassurances. "Be well," we say. "Take care of yourself." "Good luck."

It is an extremely odd situation to be born and the oddest thing about it is how rarely we mention how odd it is. Logically, we should immediately direct our attention to the central facts of what we name life: we do not know where we come from when we are born, or why we are here, or where we are going when we die. It took forty-six years for me to address myself energetically to this situation, to seek information with the mature intellect at my command, and to begin to line myself up toward an understanding of reality within which a life makes sense. Now I work during a daily quiet period on this alignment and test out all that I learn, matching every nuance against my accumulated experience—a taxing endeavor. If I knew another way, I would abandon this one because it is so hard, but nothing else proves out so lucidly.

When I was about ten years old, I went to a summer camp. A few days after we had settled into our tents and made our little arrangements with the oddities of outdoor life, the director announced that we would be going on a snipe hunt that evening. I was excited. A hunt meant to me that I would have a chance to find something new. I remember sitting shyly on the ground that afternoon next to the counselor in charge of my tent. I hugged my knees happily and confided to her how much I looked forward to the hunt, and when in the early evening we were given large paper bags and placed at distances here and there in the woods I took up my station with a high heart. We were instructed to keep our bags open. Snipe were hard to catch but they liked bags and if we were patient they would come and creep into ours. We were to sit and wait without a sound. I made sure my bag was nice and wide. I sat. The woods around me darkened. Occasionally, I heard distant noises but with confident self-discipline I concluded that other campers had gotten scared and put the snipe off. I was scared myself. But intent. If anyone was going to catch a snipe it was going to be me. I remember finally falling into a kind of quiet stoicism that was half stubborn and then, alone in the night woods, into a plain feeling of perseverance that had not so much to do with the hope of success as with loyalty to my own purpose.

When the counselor finally came to get me, I sat without moving an inch while I watched her flashlight waver through the trees. It was with difficulty that I took in the fact that she was accompanied by laughing campers who were laughing at me because all of them had long ago caught on to the joke.

I sit quietly every day with a comparable fortitude, trying to reach and to hold a state of consciousness that sometimes renders me receptive to knowledge in no other way accessible to me.

22 AUGUST

The pressures of administration have returned me to the tight strictures of my situation in the 1960s, when I had to juggle my own work with the demands of a hospitable husband, three young children, and a large household. If I have an hour, I try to use it; even fifteen minutes. I am inevitably slowed down, but I am not stopped. All around me, the beauty of Yaddo sustains me: cool and shortening days, the still-subtle changes toward autumn in the leaves and the lives of the animals who are living here in the course of their seasons. The little foxes are growing up. The spotted fawns are becoming deer. A hibiscus near my house has produced a pink blossom almost a foot in diameter, so exotic that it looks as if it had grown in heaven.

The turn of season has brought me to a consideration of staff salaries, which are determined in late summer by the executive director with the approval of the executive committee. For some weeks now I have been thinking over the people who work here. In the most modest way, I find myself understanding the broad beneficence of the divine, for in each person I see a balance so personal that I respect and honor them all equally in the context of their individualities. Some are showier than others, have a capacity to lead and to grow into more responsibilities; others do not bid fair to become effective in a wider range. But the longer and more carefully I observe, the more clearly I see that there is room within the structure of Yaddo for the play of each one against another. The earnestness and immediacy of all their lives touches a chord of response in me: I desire their well-being.

24 AUGUST

I have had reason to talk with an insurance broker and have learned that my actuarial expectation of life is eighty years. Statistics apparently prove that the longer you live, the longer you are likely to live. I'm not sure how I feel about that. Seventeen more years. Seventeen years back, I was forty-six—eons ago. I returned from Japan when I was forty-six. That year worked such a turn in my life that I remember all that I felt before it through the prism of all that I have learned since. Interesting to think that seventeen years from now I may, probably will, if I live, be feeling just so about the years ahead of me now.

Autumn

The past week has been extraordinarily difficult. Something in the air has stirred varieties of psychological tension as distinct as dust dervishes. The culmination was two thunder-and-lightning storms more nakedly powerful than any I have ever experienced. One morning an ancient pine, one of a stately colonnade, was struck down by lightning—the bark stripped right off the trunk and the whole top ripped off. I reached it minutes after it fell. Its great boughs, all luxuriant and delicate needles, lay soft as shining hair on the cropped meadow. In a hideous contrast, as obscene as if a person had been skinned in a stroke, the inside of the tree was exposed in bare, pale yellow heartwood splintered in spikes that seemed almost visibly to quiver in shock. No sensitive person could have failed to recognize the *death* of this tree. I put my hands on its exposed body and into my palms seeped sap sticky and profuse as blood.

From the clap of thunder and lightning to the moment of touching this subsiding life stream, I never felt any fear. I remember thinking, "I'm not afraid." I was astonished. Usually when I have been that startled I have felt a sort of unsettlement in the very ground of myself, as if every cell in my body had instantly mobilized to withstand threat.

That night another much longer and more intense storm struck Yaddo. I was alone in my house. I turned off the lights, and sat quietly and peacefully while a facsimile of all terror screamed and flashed over my head. When it lessened, I went to the window facing the colonnade of pine trees and saw the cuts of lightning reiterated in the jagged skeleton of the great felled tree.

I am astonished by my acceptance of these storms. Long months of living in the country must have worked an alchemy in me, providing me with an understanding of nature broader and deeper in dimension than any I have ever known. I am finding myself equally at home with both violence and tranquillity. I recognize how they complement and validate one another. I feel an unfamiliar conviction of safety pervasive as an atmosphere, as if I were breathing a new air.

5   SEPTEMBER

I continue to breathe this air. A mysterious change has taken place in the center of my being, as if it had begun to glow, pervading me with a new, peaceful joy. I walk around living my ordinary life. Nothing shows. But I am different.

We at Yaddo are now gathering our forces for the annual meeting of the members and directors of the corporation, who will be coming this weekend. Our artists are departing. There are only fifteen left this morning. All will be gone in two more days. The members and directors will leave next Sunday. We then close the Mansion for the winter. New guests arrive the following Thursday, the start of the winter season, when, a smaller group of twelve until spring, we will have our meals in the Yaddo library. The days are definitely shorter and it is cold in the mornings and evenings.

I went out to dinner on Labor Day and encountered another of the women with whom I went to college, again for the first time in forty-odd years. And again recognized and was recognized, though we are both graying and a bit wrinkled. Changed in more subtle ways too, of course, but although the details are different our two patterns are not. It is as if we had filled out, made explicit, destinies that were once only implicit in our miens. I am reminded of my grandsons' faces when they were born: they looked entirely formed, their destinies writ large on their stern and purposed faces. This look lasts only a few days, after which a newly born person falls into babyhood. But a pattern remains, stamped beneath flesh and bone.

6 SEPTEMBER

A just-born golden sun is gilding the trees beyond the panes of my glass doors. They are becoming minute by minute more glowing, fulgent of the promises beauty proffers so generously. A few weeks ago, I would have yearned toward these promises, with hope against hope. I watch this morning with no such yearning, desireless, at the psychological distance that is so new to me.

New and at the same time strangely reminiscent. I have never felt that I entirely belonged in the world and have spent my life looking for subtle equivalents of what I was somehow born knowing. I have not found them except in rare flashes of insight and in the work I make in order to render these insights more accessible, to reaffirm them for myself. It is for this reason that my work feels like home to me in a way that the world has never felt. It is as if I felt safer before I was born—odd as that sounds to my ear—and I seem lately to have come to an understanding of natural reality that is endowing me with some similar feeling of safety.

My first wholly coherent memory, that of light flaring across a ceiling while my nurse changed my diaper, was tainted by an immediate recognition that I was in an alien pulpy body in an alien place—hence in jeopardy. This dismay was not contradicted by the experience of my life, which rather gently but relentlessly led me from the illusions I worked so hard to formulate in order to make myself feel safe, to disillusions. The gentleness I owe to the honest affection I have received throughout my life—from my parents, my sisters, my friends, my husband, my children—and to the agreeable aspects that have lulled and beguiled me in this world. The relentless growth out of illusion has been no one's fault. Rather it seems to me to have been a long lesson during which I have been brought to my present state of mind: one in which I am able to substitute for my manufacture of an illusion of safety in the world a conviction that I exist independently of it. It is this conviction with which I was born.

I am still watching the trees. The light is pale lemon now. If what I am watching evaporated before my eyes, I would remain.

If I evaporated, it would remain.

My sister Louise has a grandson, Daniel, born yesterday. She said, "He rounds off my life. If I died tomorrow, I would die happy."

We spoke of heredity. Louise's daughter was born with all her ova intact in her body in the form of cells due to mature at puberty. So one-half of Daniel's heredity was borne inside Louise's body when his mother was a fetus. In this sense, we are our grandchildren's parents. When my first grandchild was born, I figured this process out and was struck by its autonomy. It is humbling to realize that for all our individual personalities, our varieties of characteristic development, we are from this biological point of view simply carriers of genetic material with which we have no direct, conscious relation.

I am more and more interested by the little changes that are taking place in my attitude to life. There is no reasonable explanation for them. I am not doing anything at all to make anything new happen. Just routinely, even rather doggedly, on my regime. But definite small jumps of change take me by surprise. Last night when Sam and a friend visiting him were not in at 2:45 A.M., just as I began to fret the patterns of my customary fantasy of disaster, the words "Thy will be done" suddenly intercepted thought. The phrase made a kind of opening inside of me, as if I had been set free into a roomier space. I felt its air around me, even seemed to stretch, as if psychic arms and legs had been cramped. A taste of genuine humility, perhaps, for as I lay on my back under my warm covers and relaxed into this new place, I came quietly to accept that I cannot, and do not, and am unlikely ever to, know how to will the good. So I must try not to will.

The members and directors of the corporation of Yaddo began to arrive yesterday afternoon for their annual meeting today after lunch. After dinner last night, I took a new member around the Mansion, ending high in the Tower Room overlooking to the east the terrace, the slope of lawn to the fountains sparkling with sprays of light—artifice in nature—and off to the Vermont mountains, the whole landscape lit by a full moon. An amplitude later to be unexpectedly echoed in the little psychic angle into a roomier inner space. Perhaps the growth I have been forced to make in this job in order to handle so many new details and to act in so many new ways has served to anchor me; I can understand more. Just as a sculpture must be soundly founded before it can bear beauty.

9 SEPTEMBER

Fifty dined by candlelight in the Mansion last night. The room bloomed: soft light and fine food, the undulation of good conversation. In the "custom and ceremony" of this annual meeting, "innocence and beauty" are indeed born. I have watched year after year. Last night two friends (one playing, the other turning the music) at the great piano in the music room had roomed together at Harvard almost forty years ago. Two couples, one in their eighties, the other in their fifties, sat very close together, shoulders touching, while they listened. We remember our mortality at Yaddo. Another couple have been married only a month, are newly and deeply happy.

I walked home through the aisles of trees under the full

moon. On the way, I passed my studio and thought of the work I have not been able to do there, but on the whole I am content. I know from close, if indirect, observation how hard the artists have worked during the term of my service here. I have in some small way contributed to their achievement, and am glad to have done so, even if temporarily at the expense of my own.

1 2   S E P T E M B E R

One of the guests here used to be a captain in the United States Navy, recalling my interest in that kind of lonely leadership. I have learned a little about it here and am no longer curious. If Yaddo were a ship, I could take her to sea with reasonable confidence.

1 4   S E P T E M B E R

The deer and the foxes leave characteristic droppings every night at the two places where they cross the road winding through the woods to my house. I look to see them every morning, traces of paths crossing and crisscrossing my own, the animals and I independently about our business, as we all are here at Yaddo. Sometimes, rarely, the guests trespass on this pattern, on the fabric the staff weaves to hold in stasis the very protection that artists seek when they come for a visit. When this happens, the staff hold a disciplinary line as long as they can; then they turn to me to underline it.

When I was a child, I both sought out (particularly in my mother) this ability to maintain an abstract severity and feared and hated it because it threatened the willfulness I equated with self-definition. The artists feel this threat when I withstand their demands. But the discipline of my years enables me to do so. Not necessarily an attractive ability. And, it is important always to remember, not one that guarantees my judgments as right.

I seem to have arrived into a psychic clearing with the understanding that my life, which I have in some stubborn way held to be aloof and my own, has now revealed itself to be as entirely subject to law as my work. Age has brought with it a certain fastidiousness, as if my character has over the years so defined itself as to render me intractable to influences that would deflect me from the specific efforts on which I seem convinced I must spend the rest of my life. Consistent choices have defined *me* as much as they have defined my work. I have never seen this so clearly before. I am, and I am going to be, the kind of person I have trained myself to be. In a way that almost amounts to just retribution, I am stuck with the results of all my choices.

On the whole, this suits me. I feel aligned correctly. The weights of my character have simply declared themselves more forthrightly than I thought they would and now they direct my life. This takes some getting used to as I have continued to cherish the habit of thinking myself autonomous.

The autumn guests are settled in. The atmosphere of our candlelit dinners in the Yaddo library is more intimate in our little group of twelve guests than during the summer when we sit down twenty-six or so in the Mansion. I would like to enjoy this coziness but cannot, as hard decisions still have to be taken and a line held.

I am beginning to turn toward the relaxation of home. I think of my friends in Washington, my own house and garden, with some yearning. I now see clearly that I am not, even during this autumn season with fewer guests, going to be able to accomplish what I had hoped to in my own work here. I have reset my goals in line with this fact. This is not as difficult as it might have been; I have been accustomed for years to make similar adjustments—but I will be glad to exchange whatever service I give to artists here for the pursuit of my own personal ends.

Sam has gone now. The little studio in the woods on the edge of my lawn, in which he has lived and written all summer, has been stripped. The white wooden desk and chair are placed as they were before he came to stay. It is as if he had never been there. But the foxes no longer bark in the evening as they did when he called them. And there is one more crow alive somewhere around Yaddo because he picked up a baby bird, took it to a vet, fed it by hand, and set it free.

A lanky ghost in his red flannel pajamas, Sam still strolls in my mind's eye across the lawn from his little house, horn-rimmed spectacles slipping down his nose, word linking almost visibly to word behind his brow. He has left behind him images of grace, along with the cool scent of a young man's courage.

His room in Binghamton, New York (he plans to study at the state university there), used to be a lawyer's office. Wedge-shaped, three windows to the east, three to the west, and at the blunt end of the wedge a wall of glass overlooking from the second floor a city intersection. Across the street, the diner that caught Sam's eye as he cruised around Binghamton seeing how the land lay. He stopped and while he ate a good breakfast read newspaper ads for rooms, walked across the street, and took this one. A young man's luck.

I   OCTOBER

Cold rain hangs heavy in dense low dark gray clouds over the woods this morning, herald of winter. As if to withstand its assault, my house is wreathed in stunning color: orange, crimson, and yellow nasturtiums, royal pansies, deep-rose hibiscus blossoms, stalks of pink stock, and a spread of purple-spiked anchusa. Summer splendor that foils the somber woods.

7   OCTOBER

Mary and Charlie are here for a visit. We are all conversing in a new way. Charlie is four years and almost four months old. We read longer books now—*Jason and the Argonauts,* an account of how caterpillars become butterflies, Susan Jeffers's imaginatively illustrated *Hiawatha,* and *Grimm's Fairytales.* We can take longer walks too. Charlie's legs are stout and strong. He and his mother play Robin Hood in the forests of Yaddo, and my house has here and there his little collections of acorns and leaves and seeds displayed on plates.

It is as if the autumnal deepening of the woods were reflected in all our family relationships. My children are now working in areas that overlap mine, so we have a whole new arena of open-ended companionship. Alexandra is evolving a business for herself: the cataloging of art collections, and photographic research. Both Mary and Sam are writing steadily. They read their work to one another and to me. We all now speak more or less as peers, comparing and pooling our points of view, reflecting one off another in a way that is mutually illuminating, enhanced by the particular bond of our common blood and our common history as a family. Mary has taken a term off from her work toward a graduate degree in writing at Columbia University and is editing a magazine, partly to earn money for her support and the support of her son and partly to take a breath away from academia; one of her stories has been published. Sam has begun to study medieval English at New York State University at Binghamton, as well as to participate in a poetry workshop. Each of us is on a distinct path along which we are walking into our futures.

We also talk over our past. Whatever mistakes parents make in bringing up their children emerge into unambiguous light if the parents live long enough to learn how their children gauge their childhoods. This reinterpretation of the past inevitably has discomforting aspects for us all, but we are as a family fortunate because they are happily mitigated by our mutual desire to understand ourselves. The most painful fact I have to grasp is that parental protection is an impossibility. It is also counterproductive: I cannot in honesty wish to deprive my children of the particular knowledge they can garner only from making their own decisions, and their own mistakes. No matter how much I love my children, I can merely continue to keep them company in their lives. And we all occasionally feel the chill breath of our inevitable separation by way of death.

My empathy with the natural world around me is deepening as winter approaches. My sense of being a mote in a not-quite-comprehensible pattern is reenforced by the glory of the forest here. Trees are the protagonists of Yaddo. I find myself more and more attuned to them. The continuity I apprehended only dimly last spring in their leafing is emphasized by the drop of leaves that is once again revealing the skeletal structure that staunchly stands from season to season—metaphor of that part of ourselves that survives all change.

We are in full Indian summer. The killing frost of a few weeks ago heralded a final blaze of vitality in which the leaves stand forth in their own true colors just before they drop to replenish the earth. I watch them fall, following their turn and twist as if I were myself twirling in the currents of air. When they reach the earth they lose individuality, are no longer distinct, but they have been distinct. I watched them grow last spring.

As I walk around the lakes, I am struck once again by Cézanne's genius; no other artist caught the implicit unity of landscape into visibility so accurately. Brilliant reds and yellows are locked in place against the blue sky by the variegated greens of the pines. I am dazzled by a perfection so whole and natural that I receive it as a given.

As I am receiving into new understanding my own whole life. I notice in myself a reluctance to interfere in any way with these harmonious autumn woods. In contrast to Charlie, I neither pick anything up nor touch it. I simply look. If I were waking up in the West House turret room I have been given when at Yaddo as a guest, I do not think I would now be inclined to line up the trunks of the trees into proportions of my own choice. Everything I see seems to me perfectly placed.

This new apprehension of unity is enhancing the particular. Yesterday morning I walked all over the Mansion from attic to cellar with one of the staff, a final check for the winter. As we closed the door behind us, the man said gently, "I hope she will be all right," and we both paused to reflect. "She" was the right pronoun. We felt as if the Mansion were alive and we had left her to live stoically without us through whatever the winter freeze might bring.

In the afternoon, we walked the grounds. In the rose garden, the straggling stalks of summer growth are tied up on each bush, and the earth piled in close protection around the roots. Each bed is ringed by barberry bush, now red-leaved and red-berried. Near the fountain, now drained for the winter (the fish, who, I was happy to hear, multiplied mightily during the summer, have been moved to their spring-fed pond), a tall shagbark hickory rears into the air; its trunk is purplish, like the angophora trees in Australia. On the wide east lawn stretching from the Mansion to the fountain, new grass is growing over the weep pipe we recently put in to drain off underground water. A black cherry has rooted in a crevice in a locust's trunk and is literally growing out of its heart. A cucumber tree, rare in this part of the world, bears the conical buds of next spring. A tulip poplar is budded too. The smoke tree's lovely tassels are tattered. Finally, we paused for a moment in the late-afternoon sun under the great stands of Norway spruce as we had stood outside the Mansion that morning, in silence.

As I walked over here to my studio under the dawn stars

—Orion strides the sky, companionable as ever—two questions slanted across my mind. The unity that I am feeling is the one I have been striving to render visible in my work for years and years. I have wrung it out of my life as I used to churn cream out of thin milk on my aunt's farm in Virginia when I was a girl. Now that I am living its reality daily, absorbed in it and by it, will I continue to be motivated in the future?

And has Yaddo's staunch continuity in historical time— an echo of the continuity I found in Europe—given me a framework of security within which I have been enabled to come to this unity? Spencer and Katrina Trask, who founded Yaddo, intended it to last forever. They built for posterity, like the people who in the eighteenth century built on their new land the houses in which I grew up, and on the structural features of which I founded my work in art. A theme in my life has come full circle here.

I am tired. It is the end of the day. I have just finished a difficult passage of glazing. I can do no more. Not even "one more coat."

2 0   O C T O B E R

My twin sisters were born sixty-two years ago today, making me an "oldest child." That's what my parents began to call me: "our oldest child"—and I accepted the position, trying to live up to its mysterious responsibility. So the birth of my sisters when I was eighteen months old activated one of the patterns of my life: a definition of me followed by my effort to meet the responsibility of that definition. I have found it necessary to resist these definitions when they are not in accord with what I know to be true of myself or with my purposes. I more and more define myself out of my own experience and find this position strengthening.

Conventional definitions can be economical, however; a decent respect for custom is not only considerate but also timesaving because it allows a pursuit of personal ends without undue friction. But I remember, sadly, that in my marriage I relied on convention too much: I naively decided that James and I would be married forever and ever, and that was that. I thought I could turn my attention to other matters, and I did. I became more and more emotionally independent of my marriage, and as I did so deprived it of a lot of my vital energy.

Yesterday I stood under an oak tree near my studio. I watched the leaves fall and as I watched began to hear the touch of leaf on leaf, sibilant finality. Just so my marriage ended: one dry sound cascading into another—until silence.

2 I   O C T O B E R

Jupiter and Mars are so aligned that despite unimaginable stretches of space between their orbits they look close together, low in the southern quadrant of the sky. The moon is sickle; against it the shadow of the earth is plainly a shadow, even just perceptibly fringed. Our physical placement is certainly odd. But it is a grand conception: spinning balls spinning around one another, precisely magnetized, always, always moving in order. I am glad to be in it.

The leaves I listened to yesterday I scuffle through today. Here and there, a few crowns of scarlet and gold rear up between the evergreen treetops and the sky. The Norway spruce has won my heart. It gracefully dips down to the ground and when its branches become too heavy it simply rises again in new arcs that extend out and up to make a new shape.

Almost all the leaves have dropped and are already, in chill autumnal rain, merging with the earth. The air is as sweet as spice. I sense an increase in the density of the earth's gravity, as if it were drawing a deep breath to be held until the expiration of spring.

In the curious way in which human rhythms reflect those of nature, we are working in the office on the budget for next year, drawing ourselves together to plan for another annual turn of Yaddo's preservation and development. In my early months here, this job would have appalled me: lines and lines of figures, some of daunting amounts; decisions of priorities; the difficult, ever-present recognition of financial restraint in the face of the as-ever-present need for maintenance and restoration.

When I decided in my twenties to leave the field of psychology, it was partly because of my reluctance to undertake the role of the Dutch boy who on a solitary walk noticed a leak in the dike, put his finger in the cold little hole and for hours into night held back the sea that otherwise would have inundated the inhabited land. I did not choose to spend my life holding people's pain at bay without being able finally to mend it. I am more patient now. We are all like the Dutch boy: we keep things going.

The land at Yaddo covers a maze of underground springs from which, by way of a complicated and fascinating system of pipes and pumps, we derive the water we use. I sometimes wonder whether one of the factors contributing to my change here is that I am drinking the water that rises from the ground under my feet.

It occurs to me that water could be considered to be intelligent: it seeks its own level, imposes on itself its own order. Water could even be thought of as more intelligent than human beings in that it behaves in accordance with its intrinsic nature, whereas we invent for our behavior more or less arbitrary rationales that do not necessarily accord with our nature.

On time, for example, we impose a grid of invented units —seconds, minutes, hours, days, months, years. We draw lines of latitude and longitude up and down and around the face of the earth. These are useful conventions, but we tend to become so accustomed to them, as we can to those in our personal lives, that we mistake these mechanical systems we have ourselves devised for reality itself. In effect, we make a work of art and impose it on the earth and on ourselves: we live our lives in accordance with our own art.

The way in which water seeks its own level, levels itself off in an adjustment that is an authentic expression of its very nature, is analogous to a way in which we can live our lives if we are willing to persevere consistently in attentive loyalty to our individuality. By keeping on being what we most intimately are, we can continually redefine ourselves so that we become what we have not before been able to be. If we live this way, we surprise ourselves.

28 OCTOBER

Clement Greenberg once remarked that most artists of great achievement have had "a friend," someone who consistently kept the artist company, bearing in hand the gift of faith, along with other psychological, physical, and financial sustenance. I have not had a friend like that. Instead, I have tried to form such an ally within myself, out of myself. This effort may have in an ancillary way undermined my effectiveness, particularly as it had to be combined with the effort I have had to make to meet other responsibilities.

Art is jealous. For its ultimate realization, it demands all. I have given it all while I was working—in that I have not failed—but I did not choose art alone. In point of fact, I did not "choose" art at all. I came to it in the natural course of my development and when, in 1961, it suddenly swelled to so major a proportion in my life, I was taken by surprise. It is startling how stealthily we develop behind our own backs. So I was not entirely prepared to be an artist when I found that I was one, and I had to improvise support for myself. When, in 1963, I had my first exhibit at the André Emmerich Gallery in New York, I also had to adjust to the demands involved in being an exhibited artist—the interface between the work I made in my sequestered studio and the public who responded to it. I suddenly found myself in a position that dismayed me. It was what I used to feel as an adventurous child when I had joyfully climbed a tree and then from its upper branches looked back at the ground, not sure how to climb down in safety. This feeling tinctured my dealings with the art world for a long time.

Insecurity is not good for people. Aesop was right in his fable: the Sun and the Wind decide to see which of them is strong enough to make a walking man drop his cloak; the Wind blows—the man draws it closer; the Sun shines—he lets it fall and stands free in the warmth. Security leads to freedom, and freedom is one of the conditions of growth.

I have been turning all this over in my mind because Yaddo's role in the lives of artists is that of the Sun. An artist arrives here into an atmosphere of support, and prospers.

Although I have not done all the work in my studio that I had planned to do, I too have prospered. I rose out of sleep this morning on the crest of such energy as I have not felt since my twenties. It is as if the young woman I once was, the one who walked beside me on my visit to Bryn Mawr last November, has somehow continued to flourish, undaunted.

The foxes have gone to earth and the deer have retreated into the woods. A squirrel has apparently won some territorial fight and taken command of my lawn. The youngest-looking animal I have ever seen on its feet, a tiny gray body foraying here and there pulling a bristling bronze tail so urgently that it sways behind like the wake of a comet.

The burnishing glow of autumn light is slowly bleaching to a pure clarity. Under its unelaborating rays, the woods are darkening toward umbers and mordant greens laced with raspberry, like the Beauce woods I saw last January on the way to Chartres. Each morning the grass is tufted with frost. Almost all the leaves have been blown clear away. Where they remain, they have bunched into clusters of decayed vegetation hanging like coarse bags among lower branches. Remnants of glorious spring and summer, they mark the history of the tree's seasons.

Come now myself to the late autumn of my life, I too am hung with its history. Certain parts of my personality remain intractable. I do not see them changing by way of any effort I can make. And when I come to die, I will die with the detritus of my history: the decay of mistakes made, of promises unfulfilled. I see this fact clearly, but with a profound, contented acceptance that in a mysterious way harmoniously contains it.

Today is the third anniversary of James's death. Enormous flakes of snow are falling deliberately through the dark morning air, each separated from another by five or so inches. I watch them drop, one by one, as I watched the leaves a month ago.

I have been sick with a virus. For a little while I wondered if the balance of my body were ever going to right itself. In my discouragement, I came to understand a fraction of James's state of mind, to feel how dreary, continuous illness might stiffen into a scab from which it might seem that only violence could rid you. Healing was a blessing he was denied. And a blessing I have been granted in abundance all my life, springs that have bathed away bitterness.

A pale sickle moon hangs like a tender promise in the shining dawn of this Thanksgiving Day. I am so thankful to have lived into the beginning of old age, for I am coming to understand its usefulness. It seems to me that I am aging into impersonality, as if I were slowly and in the most ordinary way becoming valuable, my personal experience so objectified by its years that it is accessible to others without much engagement of my ego. I have noticed this kind of impersonal distance in people older than I, and wondered what it would feel like, and now I know, and I like it.

A goodly part of this impersonality has been conferred on me during these months of service at Yaddo, for here I have been privileged to learn enough about a particular piece of land to understand the union that illuminates the symbiosis of humankind with the earth. From ruby dawn to amber dusk, I note the earth's rich changes and feel them reverberate within me as if I were a tuning fork.

Sam and Mary and Charlie are here for Thanksgiving. We walk around the lakes every afternoon. Mary wears a red woolen band around her yellow hair and Charlie a red down jacket. Sam's coat is brown-checked with a shawl collar of woolly stuff. I seem to myself invisible. They scoot up and slide down the wooded hills and cross the streams on logs. The ice on the lakes is like a lid that lifts as a whole when they press their feet on its edge, and slaps down with a smart bark. They break off pieces of its rim and skip them over the frozen surface. We are enchanted by the sound as the fragments strike and scatter, sharp cracks skidding into a diminishing echo we listen to until we can hear no more.

Winter

Curtis Harnack has returned from Italy. We met yesterday in New York City. In almost five hours of deliberate and compatible discourse, I poured Yaddo back into his open hands. When we parted, I put on my thick tweed coat and walked in the frosty air up and down alongside the twinkling Christmas trees lining Park Avenue, my hands carelessly in my pockets and my hair ruffling in the night wind.

I am preparing to leave Yaddo. My sculptures have gone, and some of my household things too. My Washington house is being repaired and repainted. I am neither eager to go, nor reluctant. I am content to know that when I depart over the causeway and out between the granite gate pillars, Yaddo will close behind me, intact, as if I had never lived here.

The earth is hastening toward the winter solstice. A thaw has peeled back the ice from the edges of one lake, revealing it to be encircled by viridian grasses keeping themselves alive for spring. Fog gives way to mist and mist succumbs to fog. Where the earth is clear of snow, its pungent smell is the very meaning of promise.

The other day I came upon an acorn Charlie must have brought into my house. I am holding it in my left hand as I write. Slightly larger than the nail of my little finger, its blunt stem tapers to a point the shape of a Sumerian temple. Narrow streaks of palest black brush its oval length under a blush of tan that deepens toward autumnal red at its tip. I think to take it home and plant it in my backyard. I would perhaps live to see it a foot or so high. I visualize it growing in the clearing between my garden fence and my studio. I see how when the fence and the studio were long gone it would live on at the particular cross of longitude and latitude where the light there would by that time belong to it as it belongs to me, by right of placement. All this is as clear as a film before my eyes—but I will not take the acorn home.

I am beginning to understand that the detached independence I am feeling has always subtly underlain my life and work. My life, because I have never quite lost an ingrained conviction that I do not belong in the world, and have never ceased to search for what I somehow was born knowing. My work, because I never have had a sustained interest in documenting the world. In 1961, impelled by the force of my childhood memories, I made one fence, delicately altered toward what I felt to be the essence of fence. But I immediately left behind the appearance of fence for ever less referential art. I began to isolate a reality of proportion and color which I see gleaming behind the objective world. I have had only glimpses of this other reality. I have made things in an attempt to render it more visible.

Predawn dark is impenetrable this morning. I see only shadows, by star light and snow light. The sun will be at its most southerly point in the sky on this shortest day of the year when the earth in its orbit reaches the winter solstice.

Snow fell all night. It lies banked against my house and stretches smoothly over the ups and downs of the land I have walked for nine months. I can scarcely pick out the stump of the tree that last July was felled by lightning; its great raw splintered trunk, its rich cascading needles are visible only to my inner eye. Ice sheathes every twig of every tree, refracting the sky, which is a silky gray, slightly iridescent.

The earth is still, spring coiled silently in its core.